Metropolitan
FRONTIERS

Metropolitan FRONTIERS

A SHORT HISTORY OF ATLANTA

Darlene R. Roth and Andy Ambrose
ATLANTA HISTORY CENTER

LONGSTREET PRESS, INC.
Atlanta, Georgia

Research Assistance
Gail d'Avino
Jason Loviglio
Eric Guthey
Maureen Carroll
Jennifer West

Photo Research
Jennifer West
Laurin Blanks

Photographer
William F. Hull

Text Editor
Kimberly S. Blass

Published by
LONGSTREET PRESS, INC.
A subsidiary of Cox Newspapers,
A subsidiary of Cox Enterprises, Inc.
2140 Newmarket Parkway
Suite 118
Marietta, GA   30067

Printed in the United States of America
1st printing 1996
Library of Congress Catalog Card Number: 95-82239
ISBN 1-56352-284-5

Cover design by Elaine Streithof
Book design by Neil Hollingsworth

Cover photograph: Untitled painting by artist/historian Wilbur Kurtz, 1927, for the Chamber of Commerce Forward Atlanta Campaign, from the Atlanta History Center Library/Archives.

Photographs throughout the book are from the Atlanta History Center Library/Archives unless otherwise noted.

Once upon a time
it happened that there was this spot on the map
that some people came to call Atlanta.
Pretty soon some more people came and made the spot bigger.
Then it grew bigger and bigger.
And then bigger and bigger.
And that is about the size of it up to this morning.

—From "Kid's View of Georgia,"
by Harold Dunn, *AAA Going Places*
(Quoted with permission of the author)

CONTENTS

Metropolitan Frontiers advertises itself as a short history of Atlanta, but it could just as well say that it is a comprehensive account of the city's growth. It comprehends the complex history of Atlanta in ways that no previous accounts have done. Atlanta's histories have mirrored the social, economic, and political life of the city: they have been divided along the color line.

Illustrated viewbooks of Atlanta and official histories, such as E. Y. Clarke's *Illustrated History of Atlanta* (1877), reflected the accomplishments of white business leaders. E. R. Carter attempted to redress this imbalance in 1894 with the publication of *The Black Side*, an account of leading ministers and educators within the city's African American community. Both black and white histories presented a past in which civic accomplishments predominated. Until now, there has been no quick overview of the city's past bridging the racial divide and detailing the blemishes as well as the beauty. Indeed, this short history places Indian removal, labor unrest, Jim Crow, and civil rights demonstrations in proper historical context.

An additional strength of *Metropolitan Frontiers* is its origin as a permanent exhibit of the Atlanta History Center. By using artifacts, paintings, photographs, documents, and objects, the exhibit offers touchstones that can transport the viewer to earlier times and places. A bowl carved by Native Americans from the soft stone of Soapstone Ridge, a mill stone from a water-powered grist mill, and a replication of the zero mile (stone) post of the Western and Atlantic Railroad represent tangible links to the waves of human settlement in the region. Each object tells a story, which is detailed in the opening chapter of this book.

This easy-to-read history makes a virtue of selectivity and uses juxtaposition to represent the complexities of the city's past. Thus, the glories of the Cotton

States and International Exposition of 1895 are tempered by an account of the Atlanta Compromise speech of Booker T. Washington and its aftermath in the segregated city. *Metropolitan Frontiers* also uses juxtaposition to illustrate similarities that existed across the city's color line. Photographs of similarly attired black and white business leaders represent the prevailing racial divide as well as a common middle-class culture.

Finally, the title of this history is itself a wonderful juxtaposition—illustrating in two words the creation of a metro region from a frontier town, while at the same time pointing to the continuing suburban and exurban expansion of what is now the nation's tenth largest urban area.

Metropolitan Frontiers is an important addition to the literature on the city's past, and will make it easy for me to answer the question "What should I read to get a quick overview of Atlanta history?"

Timothy J. Crimmins
Georgia State University

Metropolitan Frontiers takes its form and content from the exhibition of the same name at the Atlanta History Center, one of the permanent exhibitions in the center's museum that opened in 1993. The thesis of the exhibition, which this book shares, is simple: Atlanta has no geographic boundaries and so it has set its own boundaries, or "frontiers," throughout its history. The book, like the exhibition, traces those frontiers, demonstrating how Atlanta has grown and evolved.

Despite the lack of geographic boundaries, one key to understanding Atlanta *is* geography. Atlanta lies at the junction of three ancient granite ridges which bridge the Atlantic seacoast to the east, the Appalachian Mountains to the northwest, and the coastal plains to the south. Along these ridges traveled Native Americans, then trappers and traders, and finally railroads. When three railroads followed the ridges to converge at a point seven miles east of the Chattahoochee, Atlanta was born. The metropolis sits today, its downtown located on the most prominent point of Peachtree Ridge, at an elevation of more than one thousand feet above sea level, making it the highest city east of the Mississippi. Peachtree Street is a natural watershed; from either side of the main thoroughfare, Atlanta's waters flow toward international destinations—the Atlantic Ocean to the east, the Gulf of Mexico to the west. The land, while rocky, is fertile and resplendent in creeks and forests; it is also at a pleasant altitude, free of the swamp pests of Georgia's older, low-lying cities. The Atlanta area supports life so well that nowadays nearly half the population of the state of Georgia lives within an hour's drive of the city, a fact that emphasizes Atlanta's dominance as the primary urban center of Georgia and the Southeast every bit as much as it exaggerates the continuing discrepancies between this urban center and the rural region that surrounds it.

If altitude were not enough, Atlanta enjoys what might be called an elevated attitude. Throughout its history Atlanta has set its own frontiers with great optimism, unflagging boosterism, and image-consciousness, tackling the seemingly impossible—from its speedy rebuilding after the Civil War to the bid for the 1996 Centennial Olympic Games. In this connection, many have referred to the "Atlanta Spirit," which has been an acknowledged part of civic activities from the beginning and which has been captured in the many slogans used to describe the city's image: the "Gate City of the New South," the "City Too Busy to Hate," the "Next Great International City," and, most simply and to the point, the "City Without Limits." For some, Atlanta is merely the best advertised city in the United States; for others, there is a heart to Atlanta's optimism that sets the beat of this decidedly upbeat town. In an effort to make Atlanta easily intelligible and meaningful, *Metropolitan Frontiers* explores the city of Atlanta as it has created and re-created itself with each generation, a process that has not always been smooth or unblemished, but that has been extraordinary nonetheless.

Metropolitan FRONTIERS

Atlanta
The Heart of a Rural Region, c. 1800–1865

A good location for one tavern, a blacksmith shop, a grocery store, and nothing else.

—Chief Engineer Stephen D. Long of the Western and Atlantic Railroad, when declining an offer for a half interest in what is now downtown Atlanta, 1837

The Region's First Inhabitants

hile the city of Atlanta was not founded directly on the site of an Indian village or trade center (as were Athens and Columbus, Georgia), the metropolitan region, the northwest section of the state, indeed the entire valley of the Chattahoochee River had been occupied by Indians for many thousands of years. Before Atlanta was staked out in 1837, successive contact between white populations and the varied indigenous tribes who lived on land they knew by names other than "Georgia" had been long and conflict ridden. First European explorers, then English, French, and Spanish colonists, and finally the citizens of a newly formed federation of American states laid claim to the lands held by the Indians.

What is now Atlanta lay on a network of Indian trails and trading paths, which criss-crossed each other coming from diverse destinations. Among the most famous—remnants of which may still be found—are Peachtree Trail, Hightower (Etowah) Trail, Shallowford Trail (which crossed the Chattahoochee at what was then its shallowest point), Stone Mountain Trail, and Sandtown Road. Parts of Clairmont Road, DeKalb Avenue, Chamblee-Dunwoody Road, Cascade Road, and Peachtree Road follow these time-worn paths.

Evidence indicates that humans have lived in the Atlanta region for at least eight thousand years. Native populations, now known primarily through archaeology, belonged to a cognate group of Indian tribes, each of which was distinct but shared cultural similarities and related languages. They occupied lands that today would extend from the Mississippi and Ohio Valleys to the Carolinas and Georgia and from Missouri to Florida. The land was rich in trees for cover, bark, nuts, and firewood; wild but edible vegetables and fruits; fish and shellfish; deer, bears, wolves, and small animals that could be hunted or trapped. There was ample water and a mild climate with a long growing season to enjoy. Many names on the land come either from the Muscogean language of the Muscogee-Creek Indians or the Cherokee-Iroquois language of the Cherokees. Chattahoochee, Oconee, Coosa, and Alabama are Muscogean, for example; Kennesaw, Tallulah, and Dahlonega are Cherokee.

PREHISTORIC CULTURES

The earliest residents in the Atlanta area lived during what archaeologists term the Paleo-Indian or Archaic Period, which spanned an era between 8000 B.C. and 900 B.C. During this time nomadic populations began to settle down, establishing villages of some size and entering into trade. It is not known exactly when the first Paleo-Indians arrived in the upper Chattahoochee corridor, but their presence was well established by 5000 B.C. They developed a sizable commercial industry

Stone Mountain was sacred ground to the Indians who occupied this area before whites used it for secular purposes, including as a granite quarry, a Civil War monument, a radio tower, a state park, and a gathering ground for the Ku Klux Klan.

through carving large utility bowls out of soapstone boulders located in the vicinity of Stone Mountain, which were then traded for tools and other implements. Between 2250 and 650 B.C., bowls from soapstone ridges in DeKalb County reached places as far away as coastal Georgia and the Mississippi Delta.

Changes occurred during the next era, known as the Woodland Period. New cultural traditions began to form along the Mississippi and Ohio Rivers in c. 1000 B.C. and spread from there into the Southeast, including the area that became Georgia and the Carolinas. During the Woodland Period, villages became larger and more established; farming was introduced, which coexisted with the hunting and gathering that had always been a means for survival. The Indians started cultivating the familiar food items that ultimately made their way into southern cooking—corn, squash, and beans. Pottery was also introduced into the Chattahoochee Valley at this time. (Kolomoki Mounds, a group of ceremonial burial earthworks dating from the Woodland Period, exhibit the most elaborate cultural expression of this time and are in the southwest corner of Georgia.) The upper Chattahoochee Valley had heavy Woodland settlement between the confluence of Peachtree Creek and the site on the river where Buford Dam is now located. The original settlement, called Standing Peachtree (later a historic Indian village and later still a U.S. Army fort), arose on the banks of the Chattahoochee River and Peachtree Creek during this period, as did other early settlements along Nancy and Long Island Creeks where those creeks join the Chattahoochee.

A third important phase of native cultural development, the Mississippian, replaced Woodland culture in the Chattahoochee Valley and throughout the Southeast between 700 and 1600 A.D. The center for Mississippian culture lay at the confluence of the Missouri River with the Mississippi, from where it spread along the rivers to all parts of the Southeast. The version of Mississippian culture that developed in Georgia has been called "South Appalachian" by archaeologists and ethnohistorians, who have studied the region and who believe that the transition to Mississippian culture was done through invasion rather than evolution, so distinct was the Mississippian culture from the Woodland. Scholars also believe that the Woodland culture was already fading out, with only small pockets of settlement and civilization left in the Southeast by 700 A.D., by which time these settlements were no longer tied to the earlier extensive trade networks or involved in the mortuary arts of their forefathers.

When the Mississippian peoples arrived in the Southeast, they developed centralized political structures and a chieftain system of governance. Mississippian peoples lived within well-defined, highly stratified societies in which major and minor chiefs held sway over small groups of the population. The chiefdoms conducted trade throughout the continent in an elaborate system of commerce encompassing thousands of miles. Trade benefited not only from cultural similarities among the tribes but also from a lingua franca—derived from the Chickasaw language—which accommodated even the hardest bargains until it was replaced (much later) by English.

The sizable, dispersed Mississippian chiefdoms attached themselves to ceremonial centers featuring large flat-topped pyramids used for burial and religious purposes. Some of the most important collections of these can be found today in northwest Georgia at Etowah Mounds and at Ocmulgee National Park outside Macon, Georgia; still others are located in the Nacoochee Valley and outside Savannah, Georgia. Many archaeologists consider Mississippian cultures to have been the most complex of the ancient cultures of the Southeast; certainly they profoundly influenced this region. All of the southeastern tribes—the Creeks, Cherokees, and Seminoles who came to historical importance in Georgia, as well as the Chickasaws and Choctaws of Alabama and Mississippi—descend from Mississippian peoples. Georgia's Creek Indians migrated from the Mississippi Valley into the Chattahoochee Valley around 100–1000 A.D.; the Cherokees, coming from the northern Mississippian territories, moved into the Carolinas, eastern Tennessee, and northern Georgia about 1450.

When European explorers and early settlers started to colonize the Southeast in the 1600s, Mississippians were the people they encountered. Their cultures were so different from European social systems that conflict was inevitable, though conquest, perhaps not. Within their respective clans the Indian families passed lineage through the mother rather than the father, which was the European pattern of lineage. The Indians conducted warfare which was largely retaliatory in nature, intended to right familial and personal wrongs rather than to acquire territory, conquer peoples, or gain treasure, which were the European habits of war. Mississippian people depended on a mix of hunting and agriculture and roamed relatively freely over the land, not tied, like European peasantry, to a feudal system of land ownership. Mississippians concentrated their farm efforts on regional crops, refining corn and beans, gourds and tobacco; they knew nothing of European root crops or European grains. Mississippians enjoyed a long growing season and a mild southeastern climate that offered sun and rainfall in abundance; they did not have to fight the harsh winters and short summers of the European continent. They did end up, however, having to fight the Europeans.

When the Spanish explorer Hernando de Soto made his *entrada* onto the American continent in 1539, passing through parts of Georgia on his journey, he came on the heels of other explorers who had also touched the area looking for gold and other riches, intent on gaining what they could for Spanish and Portuguese crowns, stopping at nothing to gain their ends. Ponce de León, looking for the fountain of youth in Florida, had preceded de Soto, as had Vazquez de Ayllón, who came in 1521 and 1526 and seeded a doomed colony on one of Georgia's sea islands. Verrazano followed the Atlantic coast in 1524 as far south as the tip of what would become South Carolina. Hernando de Soto was not the first explorer, but coming at the end of the Mississippian period, his visit was a harbinger of the dissolution in store for the native peoples. His soldiers enslaved large numbers of Indians, disrupting families and villages; they introduced powerful European diseases to the native populations, who had no natural immunities to smallpox, diphtheria, and tuberculosis. Though de Soto did not pass through the northwest section of the Chattahoochee Valley, the area was known to him and the other explorers, and ultimately the Spanish had forts this far north at a time before Georgia was a colony of the British crown.

THE COLONY OF GEORGIA

Long before Georgia was settled as a colony of Great Britain, its fortunes were tied to the trade routes across the Atlantic Ocean. Spain, France, and England all vied for routes to and from the riches of the southeastern section of the New World, and once they had colonized the Atlantic coast, the European nations pushed their colonists inland as far as they could. As the coastal trade increased, so did colonization; as colonization increased, so did the desire for more land and the conflicts among the European nations; as the expansion inland increased, so did the need for major trade centers in the interior. A century of exactly that kind of expansion occurred—accompanied by a series of armed conflicts and outright wars, from the French and Indian Wars to the American Revolution—between the English colonization of Georgia in 1732 and the founding of Atlanta in 1837.

Two Atlantic seaports are important to Atlanta's story because they created the need for inland trade centers: Charles Towne (now Charleston, South Carolina), established in 1670, and Savannah, Georgia, established in 1733. From these two coastal towns, the English and their servants, slaves, and associates pushed inland to the west, south, and north. They encountered Creek Indians and Spanish and French traders. When the colony of Georgia was established in 1732, its founders had in mind to make profits for the English crown and thus set out to settle the land any way they could. To do so, they first indentured landless European peasants, who immigrated as laborers and servants; then they enslaved Africans and imported them directly to the colony, as the Virginia and Carolina colonies had done since 1619.

The value of the African slaves to an emerging plantation system was readily established. Planters of the Old South were land hungry and dependent on slave labor to produce their labor-intensive crops—rice, cotton, and tobacco. Once the invention of the cotton gin in 1790 established cotton as the crop of preference among plantation owners, the hunger for land simply skyrocketed, and the dependence on slave labor snowballed as well. Efforts to enslave Indians to work the plantations met with little success. Unlike the Africans, who were separated from their native populations, local Indians were hard to isolate from their tribes. They often refused to work for whites, even when punished for such refusals. Whites and Indians began to compete for the same lands, so whites used the powers of their laws, their militia, and their

The west side of Whitehall Street between Alabama Street and the railroad, showing one of the slave auction houses in the city.

words to eliminate Indian claims. And they brought in Africans to work the lands. This was the setting in southeastern colonial America when Georgia was founded.

Contact with the Europeans radically changed the cultures of both the Creeks and the Cherokee Indians, who were well settled in Georgia territory by 1733. For a century the Indians had suffered from European diseases; lost land to European settlers; traded foodstuffs for European tools, arms, and trinkets; and gotten accustomed, however reluctantly, to foreign presence on their soil. From the 1690s on, both tribes had conducted regular trade with South Carolina colonists, who were not the first Europeans but were the first Englishmen that the Indians knew. English became the common language of trade, and English markets the source of the greatest variety of trade items. And Georgia became the stronghold of the English, after serious contests with Spain and France.

When the English settled the coast of Georgia in 1733, they were befriended by the Creek Indians, who remained loyal to the crown throughout the colonial period, fighting on the side of the British during the American Revolution. In the early years of the English colony, there were French and Spanish colonials in Georgia; but after the end of the Seven Years' War in 1763, the British took the Spanish territory and the Spanish took the French territory. The Creeks interacted with all the colonials but favored the English, while the Cherokees lived in relative isolation from everyone in the north Georgia mountains.

Nonetheless, the Cherokees were beginning to feel the pressure of Creeks moving into their territory as the Creeks moved away from the white settlers. The Cherokees also began to feel the threat of Anglo traders, cattlemen, and squatters, who were pushing north into whatever territory they saw.

Ever eager to acquire land, the colony of Georgia negotiated for Creek territory between the Savannah and Ogeechee Rivers in 1763; the colony gained much more Creek territory by treaty in 1773—from the Ogeechee River to the Altamaha River, from the headwaters of the Oconee to the Savannah—land that butted up against the Cherokees. During the American Revolution, the Cherokees struck back at the encroachments, attacking both American colonials and the British. The Creeks fought the Americans. Both the Cherokees and the Creeks were subjected to angry American reprisals during and after the revolution. The Indian groups, fighting each other and the whites, passed back and forth across the Chattahoochee River, loosely claiming the land on either side as Cherokee or Creek. Finally, American military authorities established the Chattahoochee as the boundary between the two Indian nations—Cherokees to the northwest, Creeks to the southeast.

As late as the War of 1812, the British continued to combine forces with local Indians, chiefly the Creek Red Sticks, a renegade faction fighting a civil war against other Creek bands. Andrew Jackson led U.S. troop reprisals against the Red Sticks with Cherokee support. As part of Jackson's Indian campaign, Fort Standing Peachtree was founded in 1814 at the confluence of the Chattahoochee River and Peachtree Creek, one of several forts along the western edge of white settlement in Georgia. (Today Fort Standing Peachtree is commemorated on its original site with a small historical display at the Atlanta Water Works on Hemphill Avenue.)

EARLY REMOVALS OF THE INDIANS

In a series of additional land cessions, the Creek Indians

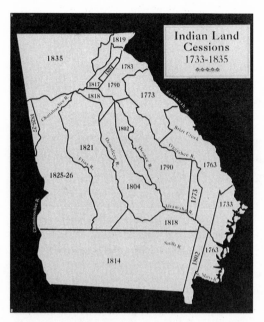

This map shows the Indian land cessions of 1733 to 1835 and the accompanying white settlement patterns across the state.

were gradually—but not quietly—removed from Georgia. They had been unable to centralize their chiefdom government after the long years of civil war and had had difficulty acting in their own behalf as a single body politic. Reduced to factions and under immense pressure to conform to white ways, they nevertheless fiercely resisted emigration and the loss of their lands. The Creeks ceded territory to the United States under what tribal leaders later described as "treasonous, fraudulent, and deceitful" treaty conditions in 1818, 1821, and 1824. This land reverted to the State of Georgia. Another cession, made in the Treaty of Indian Spring of 1825, had particularly virulent effects; it took two painful years for the Creek delegation to renegotiate in Washington, D.C., while the Creek people suffered from disease, vandalism, and starvation. The last of the Creek holdings in Georgia were ceded to the state in 1827 under the Treaty of Fort Mitchell. Georgia was now "free" of Indians west to the Alabama line and north to the Chattahoochee River—including the land the city of Atlanta sits upon. All the treaties with the Creeks notwithstanding, Georgia was still left with Indians occupying the northwest corner of the state. There Cherokees inhabited a small but important piece of land as part of their larger holdings, which spread into Tennessee, Alabama, and the eastern Carolinas.

CHEROKEE STRONGHOLD

Of all the tribes of the southeastern Indians—the Cherokees, the Choctaws, the Chickasaws, the Creeks, and the Seminoles, often called the "five civilized tribes"—the Cherokees of Georgia evidenced the most willingness to adapt themselves to invasive foreign cultures while at the same time strenuously resisting removal from their territories. Northwest Georgia became their political and spiritual stronghold where they exercised the greatest measures of conformity: they adopted white agricultural practices, built saw- and gristmills, and began to parcel out their land in quasi-Anglo farmstead allotments. They built a new capital at New Echota (near Rome, Georgia), adopted a democratic constitution based on the U.S. Constitution, willingly accepted American missionaries in their folds to teach them to read, and created an alphabet of the Cherokee language, which enabled them to have a printing press and publish their own books and newspaper (in both English and Cherokee).

James Vann, one of the wealthier Georgia Cherokee chiefs, offers an exceptional example of their success. His homestead included eight hundred acres of cultivated land, several dozen cabins (for his black slaves), multiple barns and outbuildings, a mill, a kiln, apple and peach orchards, a shop, trading post, and foundry, and an impressive three-story home, which is now a Georgia historical landmark. The house was built on the federal turnpike that the U.S. government had laid out to run from Athens, Georgia, to Nashville, Tennessee, through the very center of the Cherokee nation. (Parts of Georgia Highway 5 follow this old route.) Vann also ran a ferry across the Chattahoochee.

Throughout the 1820s the Cherokees continued to combat white encroachment, centralizing the powers of their nation more tightly through every legislative act they passed, in order to affirm their own political existence. A new court system, elective representation, a salaried government bureaucracy, English as the official language, and a move toward agricultural initiatives—all signaled "advancement" to the white power structure, but were changes that many full-blooded Cherokees resisted and many ordinary whites ignored. The changes did little to prevent white encroachment on Cherokee land and nothing at all to keep the tribe from existing at the mercy of the white government, however much "advancement" its members made. The pressure was so great, the tribe imploded. A revolt, known as the White Path's Rebellion, erupted in 1827 and divided the Cherokee nation into two groups. The nation remained divided despite strong leadership on both sides during the tense decades of the 1820s and 1830s. Division made the Cherokees as vulnerable to the whites as it had the Creeks.

WHITE SETTLEMENT AND CHEROKEE REMOVAL

The Cherokees lived northwest of the Chattahoochee River, across from land occupied for generations by their old, inimical neighbors, the Creeks. The Creeks ceded the last of their lands southeast of the Chattahoochee to Georgia in 1821, leaving that territory open to white settlement. The Cherokees were now to have new neighbors. DeKalb County, Georgia, established in 1823, was carved out of the portion of Creek lands lying closest to the Chattahoochee, and Decatur, then located in the very middle of a much larger county, was fixed as the county seat.

One of DeKalb's first citizens, James Mc. Montgomery, was representative of the many pioneers who settled there. Montgomery owned and operated a ferry across the Chattahoochee River in the village of Fort Peachtree, where he also served as postmaster. His settlement was one of the closest to Cherokee lands. Others regularly crossed the river to settle on land without benefit of purchase or deed. Though they were not numerous at first, these squatters were the harbingers of more sizable and serious encroachments.

With internal conflicts, white squatters on their property, and uncertainties about the future of federal support for their livelihood, the Cherokees faced the disastrous developments that ultimately ended their tenure in Georgia. First of all, gold was discovered in 1829 in Cherokee Territory (near what is now Dahlonega, Georgia). Whites poured into Cherokee lands, hunting fortunes and creating havoc with the resident Indians. President Andrew Jackson sent in federal troops to restore order to the Indian territory, but the State of Georgia insisted that they leave. Georgia considered Cherokee Territory to be state, not federal, territory, having passed a law two years earlier declaring sovereignty over the coveted Indian lands. That act placed the entire Cherokee Nation under Georgia rule, specifically assigning various lands to the frontier counties of Carroll, DeKalb, Gwinnett, Hall, and Habersham. The act also declared Indians incompetent to bear witness against whites and ruled their laws null and void, rendering the Cherokees incapable of dissent over the land grab. Georgia followed this law by illegally surveying Cherokee lands and distributing them to white citizens through a land lottery. The Indians, while not physically removed from the territory, were robbed of their homes, farms, orchards, mills, and small factories.

The impositions of the gold rush were severe enough, but the worst was yet to come. In 1830, the United States passed the Indian Removal Act, which called for the relocation of all southeastern Indians to lands in the western territories. The bill, one of the most hotly debated in U.S. history, presaged the kind of sectional bitterness that marked the 1850s congressional debates over slavery and state's rights. The Cherokees spent five years in difficult negotiations and expensive court proceedings to avert the new Removal Act. A few hundred Cherokees left voluntarily; two thousand had left by the middle of the decade.

In 1835, the Cherokees, or, rather, a faction of the most elite, civilized, and literate of them, signed the Treaty of New Echota, agreeing to removal. Chief John Ross and many full-bloods refused to sign. Their resistance lasted several more years until 1838, when General Winfield Scott was finally sent in with U.S. troops to escort all remaining Cherokees from Georgia lands. He located his headquarters at the Cherokee capital, New Echota, and collected the Indians into concentration camps until he had mustered enough to caravan west. In all, 18,000 were forced to relocate in Arkansas and Oklahoma, traveling under such grueling circumstances that as many as 4,000 died.

All the lands in the state of Georgia were now open for legal white development. Though a handful of Creeks and Cherokees were able to avoid removal by hiding out or passing into white oblivion, Georgia has been empty of Native American communities from 1838 until the present day, when assorted Creek and Cherokee clans have begun obtaining official federal certification as resident tribes. The state owns and preserves the once-sacred sites of the ancient cultures—the Rock Eagle formation and the Kolomoki, Etowah, and Ocmulgee Mounds—as historic properties, but Georgia is the only state in the South without a single acre set aside as a residential trust or reservation for native peoples.

WHITE SETTLEMENT IN NORTH GEORGIA

White settlement of Atlanta and the rest of northwest Georgia depended on the removal of the Cherokee Nation from Georgia and did not occur in great numbers until the Indians were removed entirely from the Southeast and resettled in new lands in the West. According to the thinking of the time, the arrival of Anglo- and Euro-American settlers in new American territories "required" the removal of native peoples. These processes of settlement and resettlement had been occurring for more than a century when white settlers finally got to DeKalb County, Georgia. The settlement of Atlanta and the northwest corner of Georgia by Anglo- and other Euro-American settlers lay at the end—both chronologically and geographically—of a long migratory process that brought white settlers from the northeastern coastal areas inland.

Atlanta lies at the foot of the Appalachian Mountains on the Piedmont Plateau, which stretches through the Carolinas and Virginia into New England. Early settlers could not cross the Allegheny and Appalachian Mountains, so they went around them in a long migratory arc that is known as the Great Pennsylvania Wagon Road. Georgia lay at the bottom of that road and was largely settled by people moving from the "Old South"—the Carolinas and Virginia—into the "Deep South"—Alabama, Mississippi, and Louisiana. The movement of the settlers flowed across Georgia from east to west, from coast to interior, crossing the rivers as it moved.

The first white residents in the Atlanta region lived in DeKalb County and serviced these migrating cattlemen, farmers, adventurers, and traders by establishing ferries at critical points on the rivers and taverns or inns along the stagecoach routes. Along the Chattahoochee there were many such ferriers: Montgomery's Ferry, already mentioned, Pace's Ferry, Nelson's Ferry, and Johnson's Ferry. The last ferry across the Chattahoochee was removed in the 1940s, and the old passages are now merely names on the roadways that once led to them.

Most of the ferriers had a complex of functions to service the travelers, including the essential blacksmith shops and livery stables to care for the horses and mules. James Mc. Montgomery of DeKalb is representative; his holdings were large but typical of what the pioneer citizens were building: two "hewd logg" houses, six dwelling houses (for his slaves), and a frame storehouse at Montgomery's Ferry near Standing Peachtree. Montgomery was instrumental in the early development of his county; he took its first census, laid out early roads, acted as land agent for public lands, served as state senator, kept county records, and deeded land to the state for a railroad he never lived to see built.

James Montgomery was joined by others building taverns, inns, and way stations on the routes west. Another pioneer Atlanta enterprise was the White Hall Tavern, or Whitehall House, once located on the original route to Alabama on the Sandtown and Newnan Roads (at what is now the intersection of Lee and Gordon Streets in West End). White Hall, erected in 1835 by a transplanted South Carolinian named Charner Humphries, served as a way station for stagecoaches, an inn for travelers, a mustering ground for the 530th Militia District, and a post office for the scattered local populace in southwest DeKalb County for at least three decades. Humphries died in 1855 and his tavern did not survive the Civil War.

Two of Atlanta's stalwart pioneers, Thomas W. and Temperance Connally, from a daguerreotype dating from the 1850s.

A second South Carolinian, Hardy Ivy, is generally credited with being Atlanta's first true resident because his property fell within Atlanta's first city limits. Ivy secured a deed dated 1839 for the land lot now bounded by Peachtree Center Avenue, Piedmont Avenue, Ellis Street, and International Boulevard in downtown Atlanta. Ivy died in 1842, having never seen how Atlanta would develop.

Southwest of Hardy Ivy's place, John Thrasher owned property on the stagecoach line between Marietta and Decatur, which ran every day; for a while his tiny enclave was called "Thrashersville." Thrasher built a house later occupied by Willis Carlisle, who opened a general store on the same stagecoach route. Mrs. Willis Carlisle, seven months pregnant, arrived with her husband only to find their "rude" home already occupied by an Irish family who refused to vacate it. The Carlisles relocated nearby to a "dilapidated shanty," which they shared with a few cows until they could claim their own property. The Carlisles gave birth to Atlanta's first "pioneer babe," Julia Carlisle (later Mrs. Walter Withers), born near what is now Five Points in the very heart of downtown.

Settlement remained widely scattered. In 1836 some thirty-five families lived in the area, which had a total population of about 253 people, exclusive of slaves. It would be decades before Atlanta boundaries would encompass all of the land lived on by the early families. In today's terms they lived in widely dispersed locations: "far out" on Peachtree Street near the Brookhaven MARTA station, near the intersection of Stewart Avenue and Lakewood, in the vicinity of Lakewood Park, on the site of Oglethorpe University, at the crossing of Simpson and Chappell Roads, in a homestead bounded by Greenwood Avenue and Barnett Street, in the Grant Park neighborhood, scattered along Paces Ferry Road, and at other sites already mentioned. These were pioneers—often kin, but barely "neighbors."

In the early days Humphries, Ivy, Thrasher, and Carlisle were joined by scores of squatters and legitimate settlers, some of whom pressed in on Cherokee lands. Fortune hunters and gold prospectors came, followed by railroad workers, land speculators, adventurers, and land-hungry farmers. More than three hundred of the earliest settlers were Irish. Many came to work on the railroads. In some instances their work was in vain: one group was brought in to construct an embankment for the Monroe railroad, which, while it ranks as Atlanta's oldest manmade structure, was abandoned by the railroad before it was ever used.

Along with the Irish, Germans and Jews constituted Atlanta's early European ethnic groups. The Irish were the most numer-

The oldest extant photo of Atlanta, showing the volunteer fire department, near the very heart of the city at the Broad Street crossing over the railroad tracks. (Note the dirt streets.)

ous. They filled the ranks of the working class, sometimes competing for work against slaves who were "hired out" for day labor. The Irish provided some of Atlanta's more colorful early history: they held the city's first recorded social event, a ball given by a Mrs. Mulligan; provided its first benevolent organization, the Ancient Order of Hibernians; composed a special unit of the militia, the Irish Volunteers; filled the ranks of the first two volunteer fire companies; and represented their constituents as three of the five original city commissioners. Catholics have the longest tradition of worship in Atlanta because of the Irish, and Immaculate Conception Church was the first of their congregations.

The Irish were also identified with some of the less cultivated aspects of frontier Atlanta—cockfighting and saloon-keeping. Patrick Kenny and Michael Kenney both operated saloons that backed up onto Kenny's Alley (now part of Underground Atlanta). The Irish made up the ranks of the Rowdy Party, whose reign in local politics came to an end in 1850. City officials of Irish birth and descent (joined in sentiment by the local German brewers) often vigorously opposed prohibition, an issue that continued to be hotly contested in Atlanta until national Prohibition was enacted in the early twentieth century.

The "car shed" and passenger terminal in the heart of Atlanta; without the railroads there would have been no Atlanta.

THE COMING OF THE RAILROADS

The State of Georgia pursued a very aggressive policy to encourage white settlement in its interior. One of its efforts was to survey lands, which the land office then disposed of by lottery. Lottery winners could thereby obtain extensive arable farm lands for the paltry sum of a lottery ticket—from 40 to 202 acres per draw. Lottery participation was regulated: enslaved African Americans were excluded; women were excluded except widows of Revolutionary soldiers; and speculators were discouraged but could not be prohibited from entering the lottery. (Speculators were apt to buy up land at low prices from new lottery winners, who had lands but otherwise little cash.) From 1830 on, Indian lands were auctioned off in the same system.

Georgia's land policies were part of a larger overall effort to create a connection between the Atlantic trade routes, anchored at Savannah and at Charleston, and the interior trade routes in the United States, now rooted in the river towns along the Ohio and Mississippi Rivers. If Georgia was to become commercially competitive with other American states, it had to connect the two systems—coast and interior. Northwest Georgia lay in the very middle between the rich western lands and the prosperous old seaports on the southern coasts. So the State of Georgia, intent upon finding ways for travelers to pass through that quadrant of the state—still Indian territory—and to connect the Atlantic coast with the interior markets, undertook not only an aggressive land grant policy, but an ambitious transportation plan as well. Beginning in 1826, when Georgia created the board of public works, state surveyors staked out lands between Milledgeville, Georgia, then the capital of the state, and Chattanooga, Tennessee, to decide if a canal or a railroad would best serve as transportation to the interior. Wilson Lumpkin, who became an important player in all the events of Atlanta's founding, was one of the surveyors and recommended a railroad as the answer. From that point on, Lumpkin worked tirelessly from his several political positions—as Indian commissioner, as senator from Georgia, and as governor of the state—to "situate" the railroads, as he described it, and to remove the Indians. As a response in part to his enthusiasm and the financial rewards that railroads seemed to promise, the State of Georgia went into the railroad business.

In 1837, engineers for the Western and Atlantic Railroad (W & A), the state's railroad, staked out a point on a ridge approximately seven miles east of the Chattahoochee River for the terminus of their line, a line determined to run south from Ross's Landing (Chattanooga) on the Tennessee River. That point gave Atlanta its geographic center and its first name, "Terminus." The W & A also gave Atlanta its first life, and construction was begun in 1838 with work crews largely made up of Irish, German, and Scotch-Irish immigrants. Construction proceeded north, but the outlook for the new terminus was not particularly promising. When Stephen D. Long, chief engineer for the W & A, was offered a half interest in 1837 in what was then but a cluster of railroad buildings, he responded with little excitement: as far as he was concerned, the place was good "for one tavern, a blacksmith shop, a grocery store, and nothing else." The demonstration excursion train ran in 1842, from Terminus to Marietta, Georgia, and back, a hint of what was to come; regular passenger service on the W & A began in 1844.

By investing in railroads, the state competed with private investors, chiefly commercial traders residing in coastal cities, who wished to expand their trade between the Mississippi and the Atlantic and built railroads to do just that. They competed in ownership though not in use of the railroads. (Today state ownership of railroads would seem socialistic.) Needless to say, the private investors had their own interests, not the State of Georgia's, at heart. According to South Carolinian John C. Calhoun, whose interests were mostly in Charleston, such a connection was desirable, and a "great city" would inevitably rise at that point where all the railroads would logically meet. Though many wished the railroads would prosper, few shared Calhoun's vision for that "point" in DeKalb County where the railroad termini joined.

Many railroads were proposed and chartered for Atlanta in the 1830s, and ultimately three were built that joined the Western and Atlantic—the Georgia Railroad, the Macon and Western (originally the Monroe Railroad, which connected to the Central of Georgia in Savannah), and the Atlanta and West Point. By 1850 Atlanta was connected to Chattanooga, Tennessee, via the Western and Atlantic, to Augusta, Georgia, via the Georgia Railroad, and to Macon, Georgia, via the Macon and Western. From those connecting points, Atlanta was further connected to Knoxville and Memphis, Tennessee; Charleston, South Carolina; and Savannah, Georgia. In 1855 the Atlanta and West Point Railroad opened Atlanta up to southwest Georgia and Alabama, and by extension the lower Mississippi Valley and the Gulf of Mexico. In the 1850s the W & A was carrying foodstuffs from as far away as Louisville, Kentucky; Cincinnati, Ohio; and St. Louis, Missouri. Atlanta was a funnel of prosperity for merchants in Augusta, Charleston, and Savannah, who traded southern cotton, indigo, and rice for anything that could be shipped to New Orleans, Louisiana, and the Mississippi River. To honor the importance of the trade connections made by Atlanta,

Charleston merchants dubbed it "the Gate City" in 1856, noting that the only thing Atlanta required was to provide "hospitality" to those "passing through her boundaries." By 1860 all but two of the South's major railroads were running through Atlanta, a signal of her expansive "hospitality" and her imminent strategic value to the region.

A RAILROAD CENTER EMERGES

As a town, Atlanta was a byproduct of the American transportation revolution of the early nineteenth century, which catapulted the American economy into prosperity through railroading and canal building. Atlanta was virtually incidental to the planning of outside agents, bringing railroads from the state of Georgia and from other cities and states in the Union. Cooperation between railroads was a rare occurrence, but the Central of Georgia, which favored trade in Savannah; the Georgia Railroad, which favored Augusta; the Monroe, which favored Macon; and the W & A, which favored Chattanooga, created a union in Atlanta that was unique. In the cutthroat railroad-building environment, Atlanta, the place of mutual commerce, was a beneficiary of outsiders' greed. At first, local merchants did not benefit as much from the rail connections as did merchants in connecting towns, yet they prospered.

Local efforts to underwrite competing railroads, however, were not successful. Several Atlantans attempted to establish locally chartered railroads but to no avail. The Georgia Air Line, chartered by Jonathan Norcross, was intended to go to South Carolina. The cost for such a rail line was beyond his individual capabilities, and potential co-investors favored different destinations: Lemuel P. Grant, for instance, wanted to support the Georgia Western Railroad to New Orleans because he already had stock in railroads in South Carolina. Ultimately, both lines—the Georgia Western and the Georgia Air Line—were built, but only after the Civil War and without Atlanta money. Atlanta became a railroad center with no local control over the railroads.

A TOWN IS LAID OUT

The geographic center of the city of Terminus was staked out in 1837 as the end of the W & A Railroad, a point fourteen hundred feet west of the present geographic center of Atlanta.

Atlanta's first official map was drawn by civil engineer Edward A. Vincent in 1853. The geographic center of the city lies not at the intersection of the four original land lots but at the car shed, the dark rectangle in the corner of Land Lot 77, in the very center of the circle that demarcates the city limits.

The zero-mile demarcation was moved east when the State of Georgia accepted an offer from Samuel Mitchell, a wealthy farmer from Pike County, Georgia, born in Londonderry, Ireland, to take five acres of Land Lot 77, which Mitchell owned in its entirety, for service buildings for its railroad. Part of the acreage was set aside for "State Square," a rectangular plaza of land bounded by Central Avenue and Pryor, Alabama, and Decatur Streets, upon which were built the first passenger terminal, railroad shops, and a roundhouse. Samuel Mitchell had the remainder of Land Lot 77 surveyed and laid out into town lots.

Adjacent land lot owners followed Mitchell's example and had their land lots platted: Judge Reuben Cone of Decatur owned Land Lot 78, Lemuel P. Grant owned Land Lot 52, and the estate of Hardy Ivy owned Land Lot 51. Together these four land lots comprise the original central section of Atlanta. Allen Pryor did the surveying for the landowners, laying out the streets to maximize their frontage along the railroad tracks. Town lots lay perpendicular to the paths of the railroads and not to the land lot lines or the paths of the public highways already in existence—Peachtree, McDonough, Whitehall, Decatur, and Marietta Roads. The grids resulting from Pryor's survey techniques are still visible in downtown Atlanta, where streets cross each other at odd angles, creating a multitude of small triangular lots.

Martha Lumpkin, for whom Atlanta was once, or perhaps twice, named.

There was no official corporate identity for what was casually called Terminus in 1837, still none when Terminus was laid

Richard Peters used the name Atlanta—"feminine of Atlantic"—for the railroad station he ran on the Western and Atlantic line. The name stuck and was officially adopted by the city in 1843.

out in 1842 by Mitchell, Cone, and the Ivy family. Corporate identity first came when "Terminus" was changed to "Marthasville," in honor of Martha Lumpkin, Wilson Lumpkin's youngest daughter. Marthasville was officially designated a post office but had no charter or municipal government until December 12, 1843, when it was incorporated as a town. The name did not last long.

ATLANTA GETS ITS NAME

In 1844 a man named Richard Peters came to Atlanta as a superintendent of Georgia's Railroad; he proposed to his boss, chief engineer J. Edgar Thomson, that the name Marthasville be changed because it was too long for the railroad schedules. In an exchange of letters, Thomson proposed the name "Atlanta" to designate the depot of the Western & Atlantic—"Atlantic, masculine; Atlanta, feminine, a coined word but well adapted," according to Thomson. Peters began immediately to use the term at the railroad station; soon the town also was called Atlanta. In 1845 the name was officially adopted, and Marthasville reincorporated itself as the Town of Atlanta; in 1847 another charter was granted, making the town a city with an expanded form of municipal government. Wilson Lumpkin maintained to his death that Atlanta was still named after his daughter, whose middle name, given eight months after her birth, was "Atalanta" (for a toddler who was as "fleet of foot" as the goddess). Martha Lumpkin Compton was honored on her ninetieth birthday by the mayor of Atlanta as the person for whom the city had been "twice" named.

EARLY BUSINESS AND INDUSTRY

The city limits of Atlanta formed a circle with a radius of one mile measured out from the zero mile post, located at the depot in the center of the city. Commercial sections grew up along either side of the railroad tracks, as the lots fronting the tracks were sold off between 1844 and 1847. Development was especially concentrated along certain east-west streets (Alabama, Decatur, and Wall) and their adjacent north-south cross streets (Peachtree, Whitehall, Pryor, and Central). In 1845 Atlanta's first newspaper appeared, *The Luminary*. In 1847 the first block of brick stores was built, and the Atlanta Hotel, the only other brick building in town, was erected. The city held its first elections in 1848, and the city council met for the first time in 1849. The charter provided for a mayor–city council form of government with a handful of other officials—a clerk, a treasurer, and a marshal. The city fathers handled all municipal business on a case-by-case basis, whether the matter was licensing a new wagoneer, responding to a public nuisance, dealing with a typhoid epidemic, entertaining a visiting notable, or meeting fiscal emergencies. Public nuisances (e.g., unlimed privies, potholes on the roads, refuse, and hogs in the streets) occupied more city council time than any other matters. The railroad crossings were dangerous; the city council petitioned the railroads again and again to provide safe crossings for pedestrians and horses, but the railroad companies always declined to help. The city built a bridge over the Macon and Western tracks near Whitehall Street, setting a pattern for elevated walkways in the central business district that continues even today.

From the beginning, city officials focused on developing Atlanta's commercial activities, passing tax exemptions for new industries, and undertaking improvements that favored the central business district and, occasionally, the white upper-class residential areas. The city's first paved street was Whitehall, though the material used, oak planking, did not last. The streets were dirty, dangerous, even lethal; in 1852 a man reportedly broke his neck falling into a pit in front of Loyd and Perryman's store on Loyd Street. In 1858 the city adopted a street paving ordinance, requiring all streets in the business district to be paved with "smooth flagstone or burnt brick."

In 1845 Marthasville had boasted only two general stores and a dozen families. A railroad boom in the late 1840s brought hundreds more residents, and in the 1850s, spurred on by local newspapers and boosters, business blossomed. Commercial enterprises at that time included cotton gins and warehouses, retail stores, specialty shops, hotels, banks and insurance companies, liquor stores, a steam flour mill, foundries, machine and carriage shops, sawmills, tanneries, railroad offices, offices for doctors and lawyers, livery stables, and saloons. Because of the railroads,

Atlanta was the major retail entrepôt for the exchange of goods in northwest Georgia and between the coast and the interior of Georgia, with a trading area of one hundred miles in all directions. The variety of merchandise that was available on Whitehall Street suggests the degree to which Atlanta filled the wishes of the north Georgia population. It was possible to get mineral water and potions; clocks, watches, and jewelry; clothes (both ready-made and handmade); boots and shoes; hats and caps; yarns and chains; guns and powder; medicinals and stimulants; copper-, tin-, and ironware; stoves and furniture; cigars, pianos, stationery, books, and liquors; groceries and spices; and livery for gents, ladies, and children. These were sold on a cash basis or in exchange for country produce—cotton, corn, wheat, flour, and meal. On Whitehall Street it was also possible to buy and sell slaves.

LIFE IN OLD ATLANTA

The year 1850 marked a kind of turning point for Atlanta—away from the frontier environment and toward more respectability. The "moral" forces won out over the lawless elements in town when the Moral and Reform Party won the mayoral election that year from the Free and Rowdy Party, and newly elected Jonathan Norcross, a puritanical New Englander, made it clear that he intended to enforce the local laws against cockfighting, illegally discharging firearms, and prostitution. Moreover, he intended to collect the taxes that were due from almost everyone. Two years later his successor, John F. Mims, razed the two worst sections of Atlanta, the shantytowns called Snake Nation (the area between Peters Street and the W & A Railroad, where the brothels were located) and Murrell's Row (along Decatur Street). The city had only 2,572 inhabitants in 1850, but the population swelled to nearly 6,000 by 1854. Atlanta was on its way to becoming the fourth largest city in Georgia, after Savannah, Macon, and Columbus—a tremendous increase for a city barely thirteen years old.

The 1850s also brought many civic, religious, and social

changes. The city purchased its first municipal cemetery, Oakland, on the eastern outskirts of town. The Protestant groups with established congregations began to build their own sanctuaries after having shared a nondenominational church/school building as their meeting place for several years. The Baptist congregation formed in 1848 and built a church in 1850; the Catholics built the Church of the Immaculate Conception in 1851; the Presbyterian church went up in 1852 and Trinity Methodist in 1854. In 1858 Big Bethel African Methodist Episcopal Church was established to serve local slaves and free persons of color. Two private white schools were founded—the Atlanta Female Academy and the Atlanta Medical College—though there was as yet no formal public schooling in the city. The *Atlanta Intelligencer*, Atlanta's first newspaper of any permanence, appeared in 1852, joined later in the decade by the first city directory, which listed business, commercial, and personal information on all of Atlanta's citizens. The Atlanta Gas Light Company, the oldest continuously running business in the city, was formed in 1855 to light first the streets and then the houses. Amusements at this time were few; traveling medicine men, sideshows, itinerant salesmen, carnivals, and street musicians made up the lot of it; the Athenaeum, Atlanta's only antebellum theater, offered what sophisticated fare there was—orators, an occasional minstrel show, local German bands, and an acting troupe. There was still no hospital, but there was an almshouse, and a public welfare committee appointed by the city council meted out assistance to the needy from the city treasury.

Perhaps the most notable event in the 1850s was the establishment of Atlanta as the county seat for a new county. Carved out of DeKalb, Fulton County was created in 1853 and named for Robert Fulton, the inventor of the steamboat. At the time, Atlanta's population of six thousand far exceeded that of Decatur, DeKalb's county seat. As a government center, Atlanta drew more attention to itself and built a new depot to accommodate an expected increase in passenger traffic.

SLAVERY IN ATLANTA

Atlanta was not home to Georgia's wealthy slaveholding planter class as the older Georgia cities were: lacking their amenities, it failed to attract them. The center for antebellum cotton trade was Savannah, dominated by the wealthy low-country planters. By contrast, Atlanta's local economy was a market economy and the local elite were the businessmen and traders, real estate speculators and railroad men, not the planters. Early Atlanta rhetoric praised the difference, touting the homegrown populace—its north Georgia "crackers," the small farmers who lived and traded here. Atlanta's pioneer image-makers extolled what they saw as the greater democratic, more progressive ways of this upstart community, the industriousness of its hard-working people, and the non-provincial qualities of its enterprise, whether true or not.

Still, Atlanta was not untouched by agricultural concerns. Its upland wheat and other products were routinely shipped to the coast, and a small, growing cotton cultivation had taken hold in the upper Piedmont by the mid-1850s. In 1850 Richard Peters talked the southern agricultural society into holding its annual meetings in Atlanta, a coup for the city. The collaboration held until the Civil War and gave Atlanta some credibility among Georgia's planters. A handful of Atlanta entrepreneur-farmers, Richard Peters himself, and industrialist-farmer Archibald Smith of Roswell, Georgia, numbered themselves among the state's leading agriculturalists who could experiment with exotic livestock and nonnative plants, fertilizers, and novel growing methods, partly because they were not dependent on agriculture to survive. These men owned slaves and used at least some of them for agricultural labor.

It was more customary in Atlanta to use slaves in nonagricultural capacities. Ephraim Ponder is a good example: owner of sixty-five slaves and himself a former slave trader and cotton planter, Ponder hired his slaves out, especially those who were skilled mechanics and tradesmen. Unlike most of his contemporaries, Ponder allowed the slaves to retain some of their wages. One of his slaves, a shoemaker named Festus Flipper, was the father two notable African Americans: Henry O. Flipper, the first black cadet at West Point, and Joseph S. Flipper, bishop of the African Methodist Episcopal Church and chancellor of Morris Brown College in Atlanta. Festus Flipper's tiny shoe establishment sat in the heart of Atlanta's business district.

In 1850, 139 Atlantans owned slaves; only seven of them owned ten or more; only two owned more than twenty, and these were both hotel keepers who employed the slaves in hotel service. Benjamin Yancey was the one legitimate planter among the Atlanta slave owners, and even he kept a dozen of his workers on jobs in town. The population of the town, 2,572 people, included 512 slaves altogether. These were not significant holdings by comparison to other places in Georgia that had higher percentages of enslaved African Americans, some of which had black majorities in their populations. The great preponderance of Atlanta slaves worked as domestic servants; they lived in town with their white owner-families. Many other enslaved peoples lived in town on their own, having been hired out for their work as carpenters, brickmasons, blacksmiths, and mechanics, a situation that was always threatening to get out of control, according to the watchful eyes of the city council. The council passed ordinance after ordinance restricting the movement of slaves; council members even tried to outlaw the hiring-out system, but it persisted nonetheless. White workers resented the presence of slaves in town; they viewed them as unfair competition and attempted to keep them from working inside the city limits. Conflict between the two groups seemed always imminent, a situation that grew more difficult to manage as the city grew.

After an incident in 1853 in which nine slaves were charged with insurrection, a nervous white city council revamped the slave codes to tighten them even more: now all African Americans had to observe a curfew when inside the city and carry permits to pass into or out of the city limits. Other seemingly petty stringencies were imposed: a slave could not walk with a cane stick on a city street or smoke a pipe in public. In 1854 the city council granted a charter for slaves to form a moral society, whose meetings were to be chaperoned by the city marshal, but then banned the society two years later. African American gatherings for purposes of entertainment or amusement required a special sanction by the mayor himself.

Nonenslaved African Americans, referred to as "free persons of color," were not exempt from the slave codes and could live within the city limits only with written permission of the city council. The city also taxed the sale of their wares and services. By 1860 Atlanta blacks made up 20 percent of the total population, but the number of slaves was more than three times what it had been in 1850. There were now 1,914 slaves, most of them females in domestic service; the census for that year also listed 25 free persons of color.

THE COMING OF THE CIVIL WAR

In 1860 Atlanta was a burgeoning railroad town and the fourth largest city in the state, a trading center passing goods between the slave states in the Southeast and the free states in the Ohio and Mississippi Valleys. Political sentiments in Atlanta ranged the spectrum, yet Atlanta businessmen tended to believe that secession could cripple their economic interests. Atlanta voters opposed secession in the election of 1860, voting for Union candidates Stephen A. Douglas and John Bell in greater numbers than for the secessionist candidate John C. Breckinridge. No votes were cast for Lincoln. (He was not on the ballot.) Until the end of 1860, in fact, when South Carolina seceded from the Union, Atlanta tolerated Union sentiments, though not always politely. The Atlanta Mercantile Association was formed in 1860, a predecessor to the present-day chamber of commerce, to promote the city's commercial interests; in so doing the association supported a boycott against what it called "abolitionist" wholesalers. Northern businessmen, who may have had some Unionist sentiments but were unlikely to be abolitionist sympathizers, were suddenly in some danger in Atlanta. The Committee of Public Safety and Vigilance, appointed to quell possible slave disruption, took it upon itself to purge the community of abolitionist and Yankee

This panorama of Atlanta, taken in April 1864, shows how the city looked before the Civil War. Downtown is located in the upper left of the photo, barely visible.

sympathizers. Many suspected citizens were flogged or imprisoned and one was killed; northerners who stayed in the city throughout the war went underground, or at least kept a low profile until the hostilities were over. Many reemerged after the war, like banker Alfred Austell, to become local community leaders.

Once the momentum was built for the southern states to depart from the original United States, Atlanta's loyalties ceased to be divided. The State of Georgia committed itself to the Confederacy in January 1861. Atlanta and Fulton County sent three delegates, all secessionists, to the state convention that voted to secede. Newly elected C.S.A. president Jefferson Davis visited Atlanta later the same month to rally its citizenry to the cause of the Confederate States of America. Davis was followed closely in March by Confederate vice president and Georgian Alexander Stephens.

Although the experience of the war ultimately proved to be a tragic one for Atlantans, in the beginning no such threat appeared; Atlanta was located far behind the lines of battle, locked away in the South's interior. Once war was declared in 1861, Atlantans readied themselves for it. Nearby counties issued orders for local militia units to be formed, revitalized, or expanded. In all, Fulton County ended up sending thirty-four

companies to fight—the Atlanta Grays, the Fulton Blues, the Atlanta Volunteers, the Gate City Guards, and many others. Fulton County sent more volunteers to war, in fact, than any other county in the state.

EARLY EFFECTS OF THE WAR ON THE CITY

The Civil War introduced unprecedented growth in Atlanta. In four years the population more than doubled, from just over 9,000 to more than 22,000. It was now the third largest city in the Confederacy; only the great seaport New Orleans and Richmond, the Confederate capital, were larger. Atlanta attracted laborers, machinists, artisans, military and civilian officials, soldiers' wives, and slaves (who came without any recognized masters).

Beginning in 1861, daily activities turned determinedly toward the war efforts, which simultaneously acted as an impetus for and destroyer of local commerce. Almost immediately, Atlanta became the home of the Confederate Commissary Department. Local industries converted to the production of munitions and supplies for the Confederacy—for example, a gristmill turned into a pistol factory. New industries were established—one manufactured about ten thousand sturdy metal pikes, intended for military use but scrapped as obsolete. The Confederacy's quartermaster department, one of the war's largest suppliers of goods, employed three thousand women as seamstresses. The arsenal employed five thousand men and women. Atlantans produced many goods just for military consumption: armor plate, swords, pistols, percussion caps, saddles and harnesses, small-arms ammunition, canteens, cartridge boxes, gun carriages, knapsacks, rifles, belt buckles, and uniforms. For both military and nonmilitary markets, they also manufactured shoes, alcohol, ink, grease, clothing, excelsior, soap, and buttons.

Raw materials were in short supply; labor was expensive, when available. Skilled labor—both black and white—was particularly scarce. Slaves were brought in from outside the city to support war production. They were poorly housed, when housed at all, which rendered their state often desperate and wretched. Those with steady occupation went largely unsupervised, giving rise to increased fears of insurrection, which, in turn, exacerbated the tensions between slave and free labor. Inflation and low wages, competition from slave labor, and poor working conditions induced labor strikes in 1863 and 1864.

In February 1862, after federal troops captured western Tennessee, Atlanta became a hospital zone for the wounded of the Army of Tennessee. In the same year the Confederacy began conscripting soldiers, compelling military service from old and young alike. Volunteers no longer made up sufficient numbers to fight. Already a staging area for the treatment of wounded, Atlanta became a launching ground for the new recruits, a temporary holding pen for prisoners of war taken in battles in the Tennessee theater, and a safe transfer point for fleeing refugees. Most of all, Atlanta hosted the wounded. So many wounded came through that Atlanta schools and churches were commandeered for medical service. At one time the Confederate army was running twenty-six hospitals in the city. When Atlanta newspapers carried the names of dead soldiers, they were not names from the battlefields but from the local hospitals.

Increasingly the social structure changed; white women took on more responsibilities left by the men who went to war. Male slaves were imported into Atlanta from all over the state to build defenses for the city, leaving behind black women to assume their responsibilities on plantations and farms throughout Georgia. Relief efforts inspired female organization: Mrs. W. F. Westmoreland spearheaded Confederate relief efforts by founding the Ladies Soldier Relief Society; Mrs. Isaac Winship led the Atlanta Hospital Association, which joined forces with the St. Philips Hospital Society to offer assistance to stranded families, wounded soldiers, and grieving widows. These were the first women's organizations in Atlanta. White women took positions in the factories by the hundreds, an unprecedented movement of workers into the labor pool.

Even as early as 1862, prices in the city were inflated, but after the Federals blockaded southern ports in 1863, economic problems worsened. The impact of the blockade was felt everywhere: imported goods (except pirated ones) disappeared from store shelves; so did most manufactured goods of any kind. Certain foodstuffs were expensive at best, impossible to come by at worst—coffee was $3 a pound; flour $22.50 a sack; the price of butter, out of sight. Several blockade running companies were headquartered in Atlanta, one of them owned by former railroad man Richard Peters, who tried to establish direct trade with Europe as well as to smuggle goods from New York and other northern ports. After 1863 commercial activities in Atlanta were largely moribund for lack of salable goods; foodstuffs had become as rare as manufactured items. Inflation was so great that some local merchants practiced limited philanthropy by giving away some supplies or by selling at discounts. Most could not afford to be so generous; price gouging became normal in most stores, while the merchants themselves faced ridiculous prices for their wares. In 1863, frustrated and hungry women rioted in the downtown, looting stores along Whitehall Street, outraged at their poverty-stricken condition.

City authorities had difficulty keeping up with the growth of the city and maintaining civil control; city services were pressed beyond capacity. The city had become a safe haven for undesirables, and some of the rougher elements, which had just been eradicated from Atlanta before the war, returned to the city—prostitutes, runaways, spies, criminals, renegades, and con men. Atlanta was declared a military post in 1862, and martial law helped to bring some order to town, as more than five hundred Confederate soldiers were stationed here. Residents now needed passes to travel about, and their baggage and packages were checked by the military police. Guests at the hotels had to register with the city marshal. Still, disorderly conduct was the most frequent cause of arrest, and complaints from the citizenry about unruly soldiers belied the chivalric code of the Old South.

Confederate fortifications built prior to the Battle of Atlanta. Most of the fortifications around the city center never were actually used in battle.

THE ATLANTA CAMPAIGN AND BATTLES FOR THE "HUB" OF THE SOUTH

Atlanta was a strategic target for Federal armies because it was the hub of Confederate transportation and manufacturing in the lower South as well as the logistical and administrative base of the Confederate forces in the western theater. One of several industrial centers in Georgia, Atlanta was more important because of its transportation capacities than its industrial ones: two of the three major railroad lines binding the Confederate states together ran through Atlanta; the third ran just eighty miles south of Atlanta. If Richmond was the symbolic center of the South, Atlanta was the region's nerve center. If Richmond fell, the head of the Confederacy would be cut off; if Atlanta fell, the Confederacy would be cut in two, and its ability to wage war would suffer a crippling blow. Atlanta was in the very heartland of the South, and if Union forces could cut the railroads, they could have Atlanta.

As the contemporaries saw it, the results of the battle in 1864 could determine the outcome of the northern presidential election. President Lincoln was already in trouble, his administration on the verge of political collapse. With antidraft riots raging in New York and some midwestern states, and copperhead rebels in the North threatening to make a separate peace with the South, Lincoln was desperate for a military victory. Sentiment for peace was so strong, a peace party candidate was a serious contender for the presidency. If Atlanta fell, the war and the political victory were Lincoln's; if it held, southern independence and peace were assured.

The railroads, which had brought Atlanta into existence, now elevated the city's significance—strategically, for the war, and actually, for continued Confederate survival. What were convenient commercial connections before the war became vital supply linkages for the Confederacy transporting commissary goods, medicines, mules and horses, wagons and carts, guns and ammunition, men and machines. General William Tecumseh Sherman, who took command of the Union forces in the West in 1864, stood poised to destroy the "workshop" of the Confederacy in May of that year with one hundred thousand troops camped in Chattanooga, Tennessee. Confederate General Joseph E. Johnston, with about half as many men, stood ready for battle just south of the state line at Dalton, Georgia. The Atlanta Campaign started when Sherman moved against Johnston at Dalton. Sherman flanked; Johnston retreated. This pattern of Sherman flanking and Johnston retreating marked the entire campaign south from Chattanooga—into Georgia through Resaca, Adairsville, Kennesaw—until Johnston stopped just north of the Chattahoochee River in July 1864.

By this time, Atlanta was frantic. The commissary department and the quartermaster had begun to move supplies out of Atlanta south toward Macon. The mayor ordered all male citizens to arms in May 1864—no age restrictions, no exceptions—but there were not many left to fight. The attack at New Hope Church was heard inside the city limits, the first sounds of battle Atlantans had heard. The mayor ordered a day of prayer. People left the city in droves. The *Intelligencer* scorned all disloyal and discouraged sentiments, openly urging Atlantans to trust in "Providence" and General Johnston, assuring the local populace of victory.

On July 9, Johnston abandoned the defense works above the Chattahoochee and established a new headquarters just three miles from Atlanta on the Marietta road. Johnston was replaced as commander, having retreated once too many times to please President Jefferson Davis. Atlanta had to be held, and General John B. Hood had to hold it. Beginning north of the city, Hood's and Sherman's forces met each other in many small skirmishes and three battles around but not directly in the city of Atlanta—one in a ravine on Peachtree Creek, one on the road to Decatur, and one at Ezra Church. In each battle Confederates attacked and Federals defended. In less than half a month, there were fourteen thousand Union and Confederate casualties. Each encounter was a Confederate defeat on a larger or lesser scale. Still, Atlanta did not fall. By

Residents being escorted out of Atlanta after General Sherman's orders to evacuate the city in November 1864.

August, Hood was forced to make a decision. His army was devastated; it had suffered twelve thousand casualties, counting the killed, wounded, and missing, since mid-July. His men were fatigued and demoralized in the extreme; they resented him and his "killing times." In order to save his army he would have to abandon Atlanta. On September 1, Hood evacuated the city and retreated to Lovejoy, a community on the Jonesboro Road. He gave his retreating forces the jobs of blowing up all 150 munitions cars and dismantling the arsenal so it could be shipped farther south and no military stores could fall into Sherman's hands. At Jonesboro, with too few men having come too late to fight, Hood's army suffered its final defeat of the Atlanta Campaign.

THE SIEGE AND SURRENDER OF THE CITY

Despite his victories, General Sherman was frustrated. He had altogether failed to capture the Western & Atlantic or to cut the railroad at East Point, south of Atlanta. The Union victories around Atlanta had cost him time and men. He escalated his efforts, committing his troops to "total war." Now for the first time in American history, civilians were not exempt from military attack. One of the first things Sherman did was to order the extradition of all of the workers at the outlying mills. North of Atlanta in Roswell and west at Sweetwater, Sherman had hundreds of women workers, their children, and

During the thirty-day siege of Atlanta in August 1864, many residents took refuge in "bombproofs"—dugout shelters in their yards—or in cellars in their houses.

a handful of men rounded up under guard, charged with trea-
son, corralled onto public lands in Marietta, and then shipped
north to the Ohio River, from there to be dispersed to Indiana
and other points north. Sherman knowingly admitted the poor
women would "make a howl" at their treatment. More than
fifteen hundred women and children arrived destitute in
Nashville on their way to the Ohio River. Once on the Ohio,
they were hired out to take the place of emancipated slaves;
some remained under the care of the army, some found work
in Indianapolis, Indiana, and elsewhere. Not all of them
returned south after the war was over.

With the Confederate flag still flying over Atlanta,
Sherman ordered his guns to shell the city. Between July 22
and September 1, 1864, Sherman's troops cannonaded the
center of town, using the church steeples and the tallest chim-
neys as convenient targets. Most of the population had
already left, refuging in Jonesboro or farther south in Macon,
Columbus, or Thomasville, Georgia. But about five hundred
families stayed behind who had nowhere to go or not enough
money to leave, or who chose to protect their properties. The
assault was nerve-wracking, dangerous. Citizens hid in their
cellars, in dugout "bombproofs" in their yards, in the base-
ments of the stores downtown. Carrie Berry, ten years old at
the time, wrote of her despair in a small diary after weeks of
falling shells: "How I wish the federals would quit shelling us
and we could get out of the cellar and get some fresh air. . . .
There is a fire in town nearly every day. I get so tired of being
housed up all the time. The shells get worse and worse every
day. O that something would stop them." In all, twenty-two
people were killed in the cannon fire, all but two of them
civilians. Among them was a popular African American barber, Solomon Luckie, who, wounded by a ricocheting shell,
later died of his wounds. The shell hit a lamppost, one of the
original gas lamps in the city, which can be seen today in
Underground Atlanta.

On September 1, Atlanta, in total chaos, surrendered without
firing a shot. Sherman was miles away at the time and did not

know until the next day that he had captured the city. He finally rode into Atlanta on September 7. Between September 12 and 21, Sherman evacuated the remaining residents, forcing them to relocate to Lovejoy, where they were abandoned. They were then relocated to Macon and forced once more to refugee. More than a thousand civilians were removed, most of them women and children, along with a handful of household slaves. The Emancipation Proclamation, which had been issued on January 1, 1863, had no effect on freeing Atlanta's slaves; liberation occurred now with the Union forces. Able black men were taken into the Union army; black women were released into freedom, to go north to fend for themselves or to remain under the "care" of the Federal army.

Sherman and his forces occupied Atlanta for two months and then oversaw its destruction. Sherman's troops burned the railroad shops, industrial factories, and public buildings. They eliminated all railroad facilities, including the tracks themselves, which were pulled up and individually tied around trees or telegraph poles—"Sherman's neckties," they came to be called. Many manufacturing houses having no direct ties to military production were also destroyed, as were private homes, despite orders to leave them alone. When soldiers burned unauthorized properties—houses, nonmilitary public buildings, stores, and churches—Sherman and his officers turned a blind eye—anxious to carry out his policies of "total war." Perhaps four to five thousand buildings were destroyed; what was left was a patchwork of ruin, described by a young soldier writing back to his mother:

From Roark's Corner to Wesley Chapel not one single house is standing. From Wesley Chapel to Billy Mim's new house on Peachtree Street all the houses are standing in good order, not one destroyed. On Marietta Street, from Bridge Street to Judge Clayton's all the buildings are standing. Between Judge Clayton's and Mrs. Ponders, I think that not more than half a dozen houses are standing. . . . Paine's Chapel is also destroyed. Mr. Peter's house is alright, but every panel of fence is gone. . . . Tom Clark's house and Mr. Cozart's not burnt. Mrs. Ware's houses all destroyed. Tom Ware sold all his mother's and Mrs. Peter's furniture to a Yankee officer for 700 dollars and left for the North. . . . About half the houses on [McDonough] street destroyed. Col. Frank, Mr. Purse, all right. Dr. Grant's burnt. Col. Gartrell's all burnt. The city hall, medical college, not destroyed. . . . The hotels all destroyed. Dr. Quintard's church is the only one destroyed. I was in the Central [Presbyterian] Church. Not a thing missing. . . . All the shops and depots destroyed, the railroad bank, also the bridge over the railroads. All the tracks through the city destroyed. Mrs. U. L. Wright's house destroyed. St. Phillip's parsonage taken down and a large fort in its place. . . .

THE AFTERMATH

The fall of Atlanta sealed the fate of the Confederacy. The course of the war moved steadily in favor of the North, and it was only a matter of time before the Confederacy failed completely. Along

Looking north on Peachtree Street from the railroad tracks in 1865. Some of the destruction from the war remains.

with Richmond, Virginia, and Columbia, South Carolina, Atlanta suffered the worst devastation of any American city in wartime. When Atlantans returned to their city after the Federals moved out for the last time, they found an empty town where civil authority was bankrupt ($1.64 remained in the treasury) and broken. The *Atlanta Daily Intelligencer* called for action:

> Let no one despond as to the future of our city! . . . What Atlanta now first needs is energetic, good government. This, combined with devoted loyalty and enterprise on the part of her citizens, and she will soon rise from her ashes. . . . [Her] citizens must put their own shoulders to the wheel, and push hard. . . . Efforts like these will soon restore her to her former greatness.

A more prophetic declaration could not be imagined. By December 1864 progress was already made: first grocers, then dry goods stores, then factories reopened. Mills hummed; wagons rolled; and two railroads were able to make local runs to Jonesboro and Palmetto, south of the city. Confederate money was worthless, so Mayor James M. Calhoun ordered municipal salaries to be paid in greenbacks; he ordered a small bond to be issued in 1865 to get the city government back on its feet.

THE REBUILDING

The Civil War provided Atlanta with its most memorable and dramatic historical moments, for despite destruction (and unlike Columbia and Richmond), Atlanta rebuilt quickly. Its recovery from Civil War devastation, in fact, was nothing short of "miraculous" according to most historians, and its patterns of boosterish commercial pragmatism might be said to have been reborn at this time. Business after the war acquired a distinctive character in Atlanta, earning the city its "damnyankee" appellation. Atlanta welcomed northerners, while many other southern cities did not. Once the Military Reconstruction Act of 1867 was passed (amidst stormy acquiescence), Atlantans cordially offered signs of harmony to representatives of its former enemies. Unbound by strong ties to the planter class of the Confederacy and influenced by those in their ranks who had been born in the North, Atlantans actually feted Generals John Pope and George Meade, the leaders of the occupying forces. Some of Atlanta's wealthiest citizens hosted Radical Republican leaders on tour throughout the South in 1867 as a gesture of conciliation, while Atlanta newspapers printed assurances of social and political acceptance of federal measures for redevelopment. The city even considered erecting a monument to Abraham Lincoln (an idea which was short-lived to be sure). The recovery from war was a triumphant moment in Atlanta history, noteworthy for the speed with which it happened as much as for the fact that it happened at all.

Atlanta
An Emerging Transportation Center, 1865–1900

Atlanta was born as a railroad terminus, throve as a railroad junction and has risen to a large commercial prominence as a railroad center.

—U. B. Phillips, historian, 1908

THE POLITICS OF GETTING THERE

fter the Civil War Atlanta's single focus was to rebuild. There was a chasm between the races; there were holes in the political economy; there were memories to lay aside. The statewide constitutional convention of 1868, which sought to restore Georgia under the Act of Reconstruction, was held in Atlanta, headquarters for the occupying Federal army's Third Military District, which included Alabama, Georgia, and Florida. The convention was dominated by Republicans who passed many radical measures—black enfranchisement, a property rights act for women, mandatory schooling, relocation of the state capital, and government inducements to business and industry. In 1871 the Democrats took back the reins of power, "redeeming" their state from the Republicans, often with violence. Hard-headed and holding the credentials of military service in the recent war, the Democrats preached "common sense" and conservatism. They were not interested in a biracial coalition; rather, they wanted to withdraw support for the social initiatives begun by the Republicans, desiring no government investments in business and decreased taxes for commercial ventures. Black voters were driven away from the polls as restrictive laws were passed in Georgia and elsewhere in the South. When Grover Cleveland was elected president in 1884, southern whites danced in the streets: their "democracy" had triumphed at last.

Whatever party was in charge, Atlanta businessmen believed that the primary role of government was to support business, a belief that has had great longevity in the city. If a choice had to be made, municipal dollars should be spent on commercial projects, not on public service and charity. The national financial crisis of 1873 hit Atlanta hard, slowing businesses down. The city recovered quickly, though, and none of its fledgling banks fell, though one suspended business for a short time. The city ended up increasing its public debt, a move that was viewed with alarm by local businessmen. They stepped in to change matters, motivated further by charges of corruption in the local Democratic Party. They submitted their own slate of candidates to the city elections, but were entirely defeated at the polls. Atlanta businessmen managed, in the process, however, to restructure city

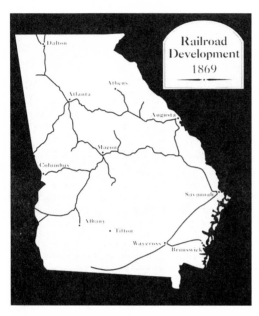

Railroad
Development
1869

This map shows Atlanta's railroad development as it existed shortly after the Civil War. Through Dalton, Atlanta connected to Chattanooga and Memphis, Tennessee; through Augusta, to Charleston, South Carolina. These lines reestablished the city's pre–Civil War status as the leading railroad center in the region.

government. A committee of forty-nine businessmen composed a new city charter which went into effect in 1874. The new charter created a board of aldermen that acted as an oversight committee for all city council expenditures of more than $200. It also took politics out of the police department. The intent was to reduce spending and to depoliticize city hall; the effect was to reduce Atlanta's abilities to provide city services and relief to the poor. Atlanta also stopped investing in fairgrounds, railroads, and other commercial ventures. For the rest of the century the only exception to the public expenditure rule was a small inducement to locate the state's new engineering school in Atlanta.

Despite the lack of public support for services, complaints from the citizenry were infrequent and not well organized, until the mid-1880s when a series of citizens committees began submitting grassroots candidates for local office. Though these committees sought to empower working classes, they ignored black voters. None of the people's tickets were successful until 1889, when the people's party swept the election, a position of power the newly elected were not able to maintain. At that point, African Americans went back to siding with the white elites, those who had been in office continuously until 1889, only to be ignored by them, too. In 1890 the white primary was

A stereopticon view of Atlanta, looking south on Forsyth Street from the railroad tracks, in 1877, the year Reconstruction ended.

introduced, which prohibited blacks from voting in party elections and locked them out of political office entirely at the local level. They could vote, but not in party primaries; they could vote in local elections, but they could not run for office. The white primary remained in force until the mid-twentieth century. Grassroots politics in nineteenth-century Atlanta never developed a well-heeled, efficient "machine," or any substantial reforms; it simply gave into business demands and racial divisions—a pattern that survived along with the white primary well into the twentieth century.

Atlanta's first viaduct, the Broad Street Bridge, as it looked c. 1875. It was the only safe way for pedestrians to cross the tracks downtown.

THE DOMINANCE OF THE RAILROADS

Atlanta businessmen were much more successful at changing the nature of city politics than they were at taking control of the railroads. The end of the 1800s saw an unprecedented growth in the rail industries, but few of the railroad businesses were managed or owned by local monies. Despite the separation of ownership and usage, Atlanta managed to place itself in a position to benefit from the transportation developments of the end of the century, and it did so beginning very quickly after the Civil War.

White businessmen were the force behind Atlanta politics; they "ran" the city. Their interests were served by the body politic no less than they were served by the transportation networks present in the city. By early 1867 all of the railroads serving Atlanta and their connecting lines were running and in excellent condition. Despite freight rate discrimination, which made Atlanta merchandise more expensive to ship than northern merchandise, Atlanta merchants benefited from the competition that existed between the freight companies, all vying for the quickest routes to get western produce to the Atlantic seaboard. The western trade was almost 500 percent greater than it had been before the war; thousands of bales of cotton were brought in daily to load on the trains.

The East Tennessee, Virginia, and Georgia railroad shops. Atlanta's downtown was surrounded by busy train yards like these in the late 1800s.

Between 1873 and 1894 Atlanta experienced a railroad boom, as existing railroads throughout the region increased their tonnage, their lines, their speed of travel, and their connections, while new railroads reached into previously unconnected destinations. Atlanta was now connected to Birmingham, Alabama; New Orleans, Louisiana; Brunswick, Georgia; and Richmond, Virginia, in addition to the destinations open before the war. Atlanta made three unsuccessful attempts to build locally controlled roads: the Atlanta and Richmond Air Line, the Atlanta and Charlotte, and the Georgia Western (later the Georgia Pacific). Atlantans, no matter what their capitalization, could not compete with cities that had steamboat connections, or with steamboat companies that owned railroads. All three proposed railroads were built, but again, without local control.

By 1890 eleven railroad lines were passing through Atlanta. At the height of service fifteen lines passed through the city, with more than 150 trains a day pulling into the terminal station. The later 1890s, however, was a period of intense consolidation of railroad lines. The great systems—the Southern and the Central, later the Seaboard Air Line, and the Louisville and Nashville—were born out of mergers in the late nineteenth century. Though Atlanta was never the headquarters for any of these monolithic systems, it was a regional office of the Southern and home for two local railroads—the Georgia Railroad and the Atlanta and West Point. Additionally, the headquarters for the Southeastern Freight Association and the Southeastern Passenger Association were located in Atlanta.

Black and white workers laying rails near Atlanta, c. 1895. Between 1890 and 1910, railroads in the Southeast experienced tremendous growth, adding many lines to Atlanta's already extensive railroad connections.

For the first decades after the Civil War, the railroads and railroad support industries dominated the Atlanta economy. The train depot was the town's most prominent feature. The train schedule influenced the public timetable for other public and private events: people set their clocks by the trains. Most important, railroads allowed landlocked Atlanta to trade by linking the eastern and western parts of the southern region; Atlanta in fact was the only point connected to all other major urban centers across the region. Railroads laid the foundation for Atlanta's commerce: they determined the layout of the streets and divided the city north and south. Environmentally, they created a smoky

The heart of Atlanta, a smoky gulch, showing the terminal passenger station and the trains which ran at street level until the 1920s, when the streets were raised. This photo was taken in 1911, when the Kimball House (left of center) was still the most prominent hotel in town.

gulch in the heart of town. They constituted an impasse at most streets, and they continued to shape the city as shops, yards, and roundhouses expanded into territory on the edges of town. Railroads influenced the nature of investments in Atlanta, underwrote the first banking transactions, and spurred the growth and nature of manufacturing. Railroads employed the most workers. Foundries, machine shops, and metalworks topped the list of railroad-related businesses. Among the support factories for the rails, iron and steel fabricators employed the most people. Wholesalers, warehouses, lumber mills, wagon yards, and stables proliferated on the land lots facing the tracks, taking advantage of the fine transport system. Because of the available transportation, cotton trading prospered. In time, cotton trading became the predominant source of revenue for Atlanta, and by the turn of the twentieth century, cotton trading and the manufacture of cotton goods employed the most people in the city. Products from all over the state—apparel, batting, mattresses, bags, rope, sheeting—were traded and shipped through Atlanta.

ATLANTA BECOMES THE STATE CAPITAL

Observing Atlanta's increase in wealth and economic position, the state's legislators were not to be left out. Atlanta was the obvious place, many thought, to centralize the government—easy to get to from other cities around the state, filled with good accommodations—so the railroads were one of the primary incentives to move the state capital from Milledgeville to Atlanta. The move was first accomplished as a measure of the Reconstruction government, which held its first state convention in December 1867 in Atlanta. Besides offering the best railroad connections in the state, the City of Atlanta promised the legislators that if the capital were relocated, the city would furnish free of cost suitable lodgings for the general assembly, a residence for the governor, state offices, room for the state library, and quarters for the supreme court. In addition, the city was willing to donate its fairgrounds for the state capitol. The city made good on the offer by buying the Kimball Opera House and using it as a capitol until the present state capitol, begun in 1884, was completed in 1889. In 1877, with the passage of a new state constitution, Atlanta was ratified as the state capital by state referendum. The city then donated the five acres known as the city hall lot, where the capitol is in fact located today, and gave the state $55,625, the value of the old state capitol, toward the completion of a new building.

The state appropriated $1 million for the erection of the capitol in 1883 with the proviso that the building be made of materials found or procured within the state—marble, granite, or

Laying the cornerstone for the new state capitol in 1885. Atlanta was made the capital of the state only after the Civil War, when legislators wanted to take advantage of its convenient transportation connections.

other stone. The cost of Georgia marble prohibited its use except in the interior, so Indiana limestone was used on the exterior. Nonetheless, it is no coincidence that the Georgia Marble Company, organized in 1884, was founded in time to deliver to the state the requisite dressed stone for the capitol. The state employed one of the most prominent architecture firms of its day—Edbrooke and Burnham in Chicago. At the time it was built, the capitol was the tallest building in the city. More miraculous, the building came in under budget: the capitol commission returned $118.43 to the state treasury.

HENRY GRADY, SPOKESMAN FOR THE "NEW SOUTH"

One of the most outspoken supporters of the relocation of the state capital from Milledgeville to Atlanta was Henry Grady,

Henry Grady—Atlanta newspaperman, orator, and booster—promoted the "New South" to the rest of the country in the decades following the Civil War. He thought the South should reconcile with the North, industrialize, and diversify its economy.

Atlanta's most active, vociferous, and energetic nineteenth-century booster. Grady was born in 1850 in Clarke County, Georgia, the son of a prosperous merchant from Athens. Grady did not coin the term "New South," but he made it popular.

Grady verbalized his ideas with wit and idealism, referring to Atlanta's phoenix-like qualities by calling it a "brave and beautiful" city when it was still in ruins and describing General Sherman—when he found himself on the same speaker's platform with the general after the Civil War—as a man who had been "a bit careless" with fire. Grady attended the University of Georgia and went to work for the *Atlanta Constitution* after a brief stint at the *Atlanta Herald.* An entrepreneur as well as editor, he owned part of the newspapers where he worked; Grady had a quarter share in the *Constitution.*

Before his sudden and unexpected death at the age of thirty-nine in 1889, Henry Grady had become the premier spokesman for the South's progress after the Civil War. A dominant force in Georgia politics, Grady himself never ran for office; rather, in the political arena he was an inveterate peacemaker. His vision of the New South did respect to the Old South while it pursued some of the talents and industries of the North. He stumped for the South; he stumped for Atlanta; some call him Atlanta's "patron saint." A talented, dramatic, and articulate orator, Grady advocated a simple program for southern development: (1) reconcile with the North; (2) diversify southern agriculture; (3) industrialize and urbanize the region; and (4) keep the social status quo (i.e., white supremacy). There was hardly a major project or development in Atlanta that Grady was not a part of: the relocation of the capital; the establishment of the Georgia Institute of Technology; the creation of Grady Memorial Hospital (named for him after his death); the promotion of the city through fairs and expositions; the building of the first cotton mill in Atlanta; the first visit by a U.S. president in office (Grover Cleveland came in 1887 to visit the Piedmont Cotton Exposition); the expansion of the newspaper (the *Constitution* went to every post office in Georgia and every state in the Union, giving it the largest geographic circulation of any newspaper in the country); the establishment of the Piedmont Chautauqua; and the creation of the South's first baseball league. He was an indefatigable booster, an irrepressible optimist, a philosopher, a dreamer, and an energetic leader at a time when Atlanta needed leadership.

THE RISE OF BUSINESS AND INDUSTRY

Grady was not alone in his views or in his push for industry and diversity in economic enterprise. He was joined by a growing group of entrepreneurs and businessmen who saw Atlanta as a potential center for economic success. They undertook every variety of activity, from making pants to selling sugared water, but the largest group of enterprises had to do with the processing of the state's (and the region's) premier agricultural crop, cotton. Textile mills ultimately were a component of the Atlanta economy that was second only to the railroads.

In the decades after the Civil War, Atlanta was introduced to textile milling with the creation of the Atlanta Cotton Mills (1879), the Exposition Mills (1881), and the Fulton Bag and Cotton Mill (1881). The first project was the brainchild of Hannibal Kimball, a native of Maine who was involved in almost all of the important post–Civil War urban development projects in Atlanta and who walked a fine line between entrepreneurial flamboyance and "cottonbagger" fraud. Kimball erected the mammoth Kimball House hotel, offered his opera house for use by the state government while the capitol was being built, promoted the agricultural fairs that took place in Atlanta, and opened the city's very first cotton mill—after years of alleged duplicity in its financial affairs. His factory was the forerunner of the later mills in Atlanta and a precedent setter for the Exposition Mills, which were left to the city from the 1881 Cotton States Exposition, for which the buildings had originally been constructed. The largest and most successful operation was the Fulton Bag and Cotton Mill, founded by Jacob Elsas, a Jewish German immigrant.

Elsas arrived in Atlanta just after the Civil War, from Cincinnati, Ohio, where he first settled in the United States and learned the English language and American customs. He started in business as a dry goods retailer, became a paper bag manufacturer, and in 1881 formed the Fulton Cotton Spinning company, renamed Fulton Bag and Cotton in 1890. At its height Fulton Bag ran one hundred thousand spindles and was one of the largest employers in the city. The surrounding village, known as Cabbagetown, was home to more than three thousand residents, the majority of whom worked for the mill or ran small retail shops to serve the community.

Cotton distribution and cotton product technology, with their accompanying marketing, legal, and financial services, rendered Atlanta the top commercial center among the cities in Georgia in the 1880s. Not only could Atlanta gin, bale, and process cotton and cotton seeds, but it could ship the processed cotton and seeds in any direction. It could manufacture cotton products—bags, seed oil, and cord.

But Atlanta's commercial and industrial base extended beyond cotton enterprises. By 1880 Atlanta had 196 different manufacturing firms, not all of them in cotton, and almost four thousand workers in industry. Since 1872, the Atlanta Manufacturing Association had been promoting Atlanta interests, getting the city to remove taxes on cotton, wool, and iron factories. Yet Atlanta manufacturing, even cotton textiles, was always secondary to Atlanta's transportation capabilities and its commercial interests. Atlanta did not have natural advantages other than location—no

The Van Winkle Gin and Machinery Company, one of Atlanta's largest factories in the 1890s. The multipurpose company combined cotton ginning with sawmilling and machine tooling.

raw materials such as the coal and iron of Birmingham, Alabama—so instead of competing in production, Atlanta competed for the dollars to be made in shipping. Atlanta shippers became expert and prosperous middlemen and retailers. The relative lack of importance of manufacturing versus marketing in determining the future of Atlanta can be seen in employment statistics between 1880 and 1930. During that period, despite an incredible population increase, no more than 28 percent of all jobs were in manufacturing, while 14 percent were in clerical work alone, to support the growing commerce. More industrialized

The machine room of the Nunnally Brothers pants manufacturers in 1897. White women composed the majority of workers in textiles and clothing factories.

towns, like Birmingham and New York City, employed 40 percent or more of their labor forces in manufacturing.

The workforce—especially women—responded to changes in available employment. More women in general began working for hire, and black women were now paid wages, oftentimes for the same jobs they had done in slavery before the Civil War. In 1890, for example, over nine thousand women were in the labor force. More than two-thirds of these were black women in domestic service—housekeepers, laundresses, cooks, and other servants. Next in number were white women employed by the textile mills, followed by hundreds of both white and black dressmakers, milliners, and seamstresses. There were almost equal numbers of black and white female teachers; several hundred white women worked in the emerging white-collar jobs as stenographers and "typewriters," and several dozen black women served the emerging African American enterprises in the same capacity.

From 1880 on, according to most sources, the commercial interests of Atlanta grew, and they flourished to a larger extent than did the industrial interests. Perhaps most indicative of this shift was the creation of a business elite, whose status was certified by the establishment of the Capital City Club in

The clerks and salesgirls at a small five-and-dime store on Whitehall Street. Working in retail shops was a new form of employment for young women after the Civil War.

1883. Commercial development was possible in Atlanta for a number of reasons, despite continuing panics and small depressions in the national economy. American businesses were becoming truly national in scope; serving so large a clientele, they reached out to regional offices to extend their connections. Because of the railroads, Atlanta was a natural choice. Atlanta encouraged this development for itself through its own boosterism, presenting itself positively to the nation as the "right" place to do business in the South. Atlanta was wide open for business, welcoming "Yankee" capital and industry at a time when other southern cities were reluctant to commit to a nonagricultural economic base, a pattern that continued well into the twentieth century.

The transition of Atlanta to a regional marketplace after the war was evident in the development of an office culture within the central business district, a changing business skyline, and an increase in the size and specialization of the style and function of buildings constructed in the downtown area. In 1878 Atlanta saw its first brick commercial block, followed by several others in the 1880s. (None of these survive; the closest example of a brick commercial block can be seen in the 1915 Odd Fellows complex of buildings on Auburn Avenue.) Between 1878 and 1892, high Victorian commercial architecture predominated in new buildings within the central city. These included a host of eclectic office buildings, usually ornately decorated on the outside and dark and gloomy on the inside. They offered, however, all of the modern conveniences of the day—elevators, mail drops, and telephones. In 1892 the first skyscraper appeared in Atlanta, followed soon by others. A handful of these still stand—the Flatiron Building (1898), the Grant Building (1899), the Candler Building (1906), the Healey Building (1913), and the Hurt Building (1915).

While office buildings grew, so did retail stores. Shopping in Atlanta was the best in the state. People could ride into town on the overnight train, shop for the day and go back home the same night, or stay over in one of Atlanta's fine hotels. The fabulous Kimball House, erected in 1870 then rebuilt in 1884 after a disastrous fire,

Whitehall Street (Peachtree Street SW) in 1882, the hub of town and the center of retailing. You could get anything on Whitehall Street.

hugged the railroad tracks in the very heart of the city. The Markham House, the National—all the hotels were conveniently downtown. Whitehall Street was the center of retailing, as it had been since the city's creation, though now it began to be lined with plate-glass windows and some of the merchants were expanding their sales operations so fast that they needed new quarters on Broad, Alabama, and Forsyth Streets.

One of the earliest merchants to bring the department store to Atlanta was Morris Rich, a Jewish immigrant from Hungary who established a dry goods store with his two brothers in 1867. Their store became legendary in Atlanta as a partner in the city's growth and development, and their merchandise was the stuff of childhood dreams. (Rich's department store stayed in Rich family hands for three generations before it was sold to a national department store chain.)

The erection of two new buildings was a signal that the same entrepreneurial interests were appearing among African Americans as among whites. One was the first hotel for blacks, built in 1895 to house visitors to the Cotton States Exposition that year, and the other was the first office building for blacks, the 1901 Rucker Building, built by Henry Rucker, the highest-ranking African American in federal employment throughout the late nineteenth century. A concentration of black-owned businesses along "Sweet Auburn" Avenue, in the midst of African American residences in the Old Fourth Ward, ultimately created one of the premier centers of black enterprise in the nation.

The greatest success story of late nineteenth-century Atlanta business is the origin and rise of the Coca-Cola Company. Dr. John Stith Pemberton originated the Coca-Cola formula at his own home in 1886, but because he could not develop his formula into a broad-selling product, he sold the secret recipe—combining coca leaves, cola nuts, water, and sugar—to Asa Candler, a druggist from Cartersville, Georgia. Candler had come to Atlanta in 1873 to work in the pharmacy business with George Howard (later his father-in-law), whom he bought out to have sole ownership of his store. Candler experimented with several medicinal products of his own before he bought Pemberton's formula in 1888. Candler sold the formula in drink form in his and other stores in the city, chiefly Jacobs Pharmacy, a string of sixteen local drugstores. He began to devote most of his time to Coca-Cola, incorporating the company to sell the drink in 1892. He used a combination of marketing tricks—rebates, premiums, special advertisements, and give-aways—to draw buyers. Candler was wildly successful. By 1900 Coca-Cola had branch factories in Dallas, Chicago, Los Angeles, and Philadelphia and bottling plants in Chattanooga and elsewhere. In the early twentieth century the Coca-Cola Company expanded into international markets; during World War II, it attained worldwide distribution. Candler made one aspect of Coca-Cola production an essential operating procedure: absolute secrecy and tight control over the syrup from which the drink was made. He also realized profits from his many projects outside Coca-Cola, including real estate, the Trust Company Bank, and the Candler Building, and spent much of his money reinvesting in Atlanta. Candler set a standard for philanthropy that the Coca-Cola Company and his successors have continued.

Atlanta commerce tripled in value during the 1890s. Retailers dealt regularly within a two hundred–mile radius; there were nearly one hundred wholesalers—for dry goods, hardware, and groceries—and four hundred industries. The retailers served country markets and other urban markets, some of them as far away as Montgomery, Alabama. The value of the industries was four times as large as it had been ten years earlier, with twice the workforce. Manufacturing was important, but was superseded by cotton processing and select other products, such as Coca-Cola. Several firms had international representatives who bought goods abroad directly for the firms which employed them. There were eighteen private banks with assets totaling $60 million. The workforce was relatively stable; strikes were rare. (The railroad workers struck in 1882 over a wage dispute, and the typographers union struck in 1886, as did the laundresses.) The fact that the local business leadership and social life were not tied to the old planter elite had made the difference. Planters were inclined to be traditionalists, politically and economically, to command and therefore protect the status quo; Atlantans were risk-taking entrepreneurs, "modern" by comparison to their counterparts in the rural sections of the South. Amid much urban decline in the South, Atlanta stood out—matchless and progressive in its economic stance.

CITY GROWTH AND EXPANSION

Economic growth went hand in hand with population growth. People came to Atlanta because of opportunities to work; businesses arose in Atlanta because of the large pool of potential employees. The city's growth was nothing short of spectacular; it grew from 37,400 in 1880 to 65,533 in 1890, to 89,872 in 1900, and to more than 150,000 in 1910. In thirty years the city was nearly five times larger than it had been. Already the largest city in Georgia, Atlanta was growing at a rate that exceeded the national average, but its gross population was still small compared to the cities of national stature. New York, for instance, had already passed the million mark. Still, Atlanta was the largest city in Georgia, and in the southeastern region, it lagged behind only New Orleans, Nashville, and Richmond—all of them smaller than New York, Chicago, Philadelphia, or Boston. Approximately 40 percent of the Atlanta population was now African American, more than twice its pre–Civil War percentage. Atlanta's large black population was making its own way toward stability and progress, with a burgeoning middle class, a small, highly educated, and cultured elite, and prominent citizens who were recognized as national leaders. Atlanta moved up in ranking from the nation's 49th largest city to the 33rd. Its growth kept pace with the national urban pattern, but was more the product of rural South in-migration than of European or Asian immigration.

Along with commercial expansions and population growth came suburban development. As commercial establishments began to expand, they began to absorb previous residential areas. The spacious homes lining Peachtree Street north of the city began to give way to high-rise office buildings and commercial blocks. The process started in the late 1890s and accelerated in the early twentieth century. The city itself grew: the city limits were expanded twice, from a radius of 1 mile to a radius of 1.5 miles in 1874 and then to a radius of 1.75 miles in 1889.

The 1880s were a time of intense residential development in Atlanta. In 1885 Atlanta's only street of row houses, Baltimore Block, was built, at a considerable remove from the city center. The row-house approach to housing was not widely copied in town; Atlantans seemed to prefer suburban arrangements to the more dense constructions of northern cities. Although the population density in Atlanta was the highest it had ever been during the late nineteenth century, even then the city lacked the structural density, tenements, high-rise apartment houses, and small city lots common to older northeastern urban centers. Atlantans could always commute; they had the railroads. After 1871 they had horse-drawn trolleys as well. Trolleys meant residents could move into previously unsettled areas, and new settlements on the outskirts of town created a growing need for electric streetcars.

A number of real estate developers dominated suburban construction at the end of the nineteenth century, two of whom had been active in development since before the Civil War. Lemuel P. Grant owned three land lots (more than six hundred acres) inside the city limits and resided in a section he had subdivided into town lots. He then donated eighty-five acres to the city for a public park near his house. Both the subdivision and the park bear Grant's

Laying streetcar tracks at Marietta and Broad Streets in 1901, showing the Belgian blocks piled up on the side of the street to accommodate the construction.

name. When Grant Park opened to the public in 1883, it contained landscaped trails through wooded areas, green meadows, a remnant of Civil War fortifications, and a "zoological department"—the foundation for modern-day Zoo Atlanta. Richard Peters began developing Peters Park on the northwest edge of town in 1885. Had it been successful, Peters Park today would encompass the land which Georgia Tech now occupies, the southern end of Piedmont Avenue, and the Mansion restaurant, which was actually built as a residence by Peters' son, Edward, in 1885.

A third developer, George Washington Adair, headed up Adair Realty, then Atlanta's largest real estate firm, and had interests on every side of town—West End, Highland, Edgewood, downtown. He and Richard Peters built the first streetcar line, which ran from West End to downtown and back, past Peters' home to Adair's. West End was home to several important Atlantans, including Joel Chandler Harris, creator of the black storyteller "Uncle Remus," who first appeared in the *Atlanta Constitution* in 1879 and whom Walt Disney made famous nearly a century later.

It was Joel Hurt, however, who created the city's first true planned suburb, Inman Park. Hurt was one of the most prominent and successful real estate developers in the late nineteenth century. He arrived in Atlanta in 1875 at the age of twenty-five and founded a building and loan association; he also founded the Kirkwood and East Atlanta Land Companies, which specialized in developments on the east side of town. Inman Park was the most ambitious of his many eastside developments; it came complete with a trolley line, a suburban boulevard, park land, and a landscaped plat in which the streets were laid out, not in rectangular grids, but in curvilinear patterns which conformed to the natural terrain. Inman Park was subdivided on land at the end of Edgewood Avenue, which had been widened and straightened to make the suburb directly accessible from Five Points. Atlanta's first electric streetcar line ran along Edgewood Avenue, from the car barn in Inman Park to the old Equitable Building, Hurt's first commercial skyscraper. The Equitable (demolished in 1971) was a solid eight-story structure built in 1891, designed by the eminent Chicago architects Daniel Burnham and John Wellborn Root. Root was a

The end of the line. The Edgewood trolley approaches its car barn in Inman Park, Atlanta's first planned suburb, founded in 1889.

native Atlantan, and Burnham's firm was already known in Atlanta for having earlier designed the state capitol.

In addition to Inman Park, Hurt developed Druid Hills. For this project Hurt hired another nationally prominent designer— the father of landscape architecture, Frederick Law Olmsted, who drew the preliminary plan for Druid Hills in 1893 at the end of his prolific career. Druid Hills was Olmsted's last residential suburban design. It also marked the end of a profitable phase for Hurt; his real estate and streetcar line ventures overextended him financially in the late 1890s, and he was forced to sell Druid Hills to a local syndicate. The suburb, platted and graded, waited another decade for the first houses to be built. Other important suburban developments at this time included the towns of East Point, Chamblee, Oakland City, Edgewood, Kirkwood, and

West End—all on the outskirts of Atlanta but tied to the city by railroads and/or streetcars. All but East Point and Chamblee were annexed to Atlanta by 1910.

The most fashionable residential sections were very close to the center of the city. A cluster of houses spread along Peachtree Street, on the edge of the retail center; another concentration of large homes lay along Capitol Avenue and Washington Streets. Highly ornamented Victorian homes were built on spacious lots, most of which were large enough to have produce and flower beds in the back gardens.

MUNICIPAL PROBLEMS

Yet even the most stylish, expensive home, with yards and gardens, might not have indoor plumbing. Atlanta was, like most American municipalities at the end of the nineteenth century, slow to develop the requisite infrastructure—especially water and sewers—to accommodate its pace of growth. During the thirty years after the Civil War, while Atlanta's population quadrupled, city services grew at a much slower rate. Atlanta was now the largest city in Georgia; it had to take its urban challenges seriously. Atlanta continued to favor the central business district and the white upper-class neighborhoods with its municipal improvements, but after 1870 Atlanta took strides to move beyond these areas. It was slow going. Street paving could not keep pace with commercial and residential growth. An 1858 ordinance was still in effect that required street pavement in the central business district, but not in the areas outside downtown. Belgian block was stipulated for use downtown, but elsewhere virtually any material became pavement: brick, stone, asphalt, gravel. By 1880 only 13 of Atlanta's 140 miles of streets were paved, almost all of them in the central business district; by 1900 still less than half the city streets were paved. They were swept by hand, poorly drained, and poorly lit. Electric street lamps began to replace gas ones after the Georgia Electric Light Company was founded in

1885. In 1887 the city sold its interests in the Atlanta Gas Light Company, but there were still twenty gas lamps on the streets for every one electric lamp until well into the 1890s.

There were no public markets in Atlanta, though the city contemplated building one. (It was 1922 before a municipal market,

The artesian well at Five Points, an experiment by the water department to deliver 200,000 gallons of water to downtown businesses, lasted from 1884 until 1894. Most of the city was dependent on private wells, abundant creeks, and springs for water.

now called the Sweet Auburn Curb Market, was finally realized.) There was only one public cemetery until 1884, when the privately financed West View Cemetery Company was formed to purchase land four miles west of downtown for another cemetery—for whites only. Part of the purchased land had seen bloodshed during the Battle of Ezra Church during the Civil War. Blacks organized their own burial arrangements at South View Cemetery beginning in 1885.

Water and sewer systems offered Atlanta perhaps its greatest challenge. A board of water commissioners was appointed in 1870 to improve the water system and to aid industrialization by helping to keep fire insurance rates low. Its job was not to provide clean, safe drinking water to the public, but rather to construct a better system of water delivery and drainage. In 1875 the city's first water mains did not reach beyond the city limits and only seventeen miles of pipe had been laid. A decade later only 10 percent of Atlanta homes and commercial buildings were supplied with water. The city built an artesian well in the middle of Five Points in 1884, but it proved to be an unsuccessful attempt at water delivery and a traffic hazard and was removed in 1894. In 1893 the city opened a large new waterworks on Hemphill Avenue, switching its dependency from the South River to the Chattahoochee River; now it had water but still not enough water mains. At the turn of the century half of Atlanta was still without water service, despite a referendum in 1901 earmarking funds for improvement. Improvements were instituted slowly; within another decade two-thirds of the city was served. The neighborhoods without water desperately lacked sanitation; diseases flourished—tuberculosis, pneumonia, typhoid, diphtheria, and chronic diarrhea.

Moreover, the city was slow bringing sewers on line. Atlanta had to cart away most of its refuse—household trash, garbage, sewage, dead animals, and human wastes. Until 1884, when the city bought land (in what is now Maddox Park) for a city dump, the refuse was dumped in makeshift middens—vacant lots, street potholes, rear yards, small creeks and springs, swales, and steep or low-lying recesses in the land. Waste was

picked up by scavengers, private parties, and fertilizer manufacturers until 1874, when the newly formed sanitary commission hired a complement of draymen to remove dead animals
from the streets and to pick up the "night soil" from private
privies and deposit it in the city dump. At that time, what sewers Atlanta had were open rock culverts; street runoff and
rainwater drained through them along with liquid wastes from
households. In 1877 the sanitary commission developed a plan
to run trunk lines from the center of the city to low-lying areas
on the outskirts of town. Still, by the turn of the century no
sewer lines extended beyond the city limits; several emptied
out in working-class areas, most of them black neighborhoods.
One even emptied out onto the grounds of the Hebrew
Orphans Home, south of the capitol. Thirty years later,
Atlanta still had houses and neighborhoods without adequate
sewer service, some with none. Although the number of outdoor privies had been reduced by more than half, there were
still thousands of surface water closets in operation during
World War I. It took the projects of the WPA (Works Progress
Administration) during the Depression of the 1930s before the
sewer system in Atlanta was large enough to service the city.
The last privies in Atlanta were eliminated in the 1970s
through projects of the federal Department of Housing and
Urban Development.

In the name of progress, Atlanta made needed changes in the
police and fire departments. Both were "professionalized,"
meaning the city abandoned volunteer fire departments in favor
of full-time, paid firemen. Police were given more responsibilities
and a tighter hierarchy within which to work. Police arrests were
frequent—more than four thousand were made in 1880—and
incarceration was short. The leading causes of arrest, up through
the 1890s, were disorderly conduct, drunkenness, and loitering.
Larceny, prostitution, gaming, and burglary were also frequently
cited in the arrest ledgers. It was rough going for the police: there
were only twenty-six patrolmen and four captains; they had to
furnish their own pistols and work twelve hours a day, and each
had to patrol more than seven square miles of territory.

The Trolley Wars

No doubt the citizens of this time felt the city streets were unsafe. Overworked police, crime and lawlessness, unsanitary conditions, crowding, potholes, unpaved sidewalks, and horse and wagon traffic all combined to push the urban environment to its limits. In the midst of the turmoil, the creation of streetcar lines to outlying areas gave the promise of some relief from the overcrowding and traffic. Streetcar suburbs growing up around the city limits did alleviate some of the press of people downtown; and trolleys were often a safer, cleaner means of transportation than many small horse and buggy vehicles, especially after the trolleys became electric. However, the development of Atlanta's streetcars was fraught with such unprecedented competition and cutthroat dealing that the streetcar systems very nearly came aground.

By the time the 1890s rolled around, the city was engulfed in a minor local civil war: who was going to run the trolleys? The city had had mule-driven trolleys since 1871, which rode passengers out the principal streets—Peachtree, Whitehall, Marietta, and Decatur. Now real estate magnate Joel Hurt owned many miles of trolley lines with his consolidated Atlanta Railway and Power Company. Henry M. Atkinson, son-in-law of Richard Peters, created the Georgia Electric Light Company, which in turn acquired the Atlanta Rapid Transit Company. Each party owned streetcars, electric light, and steam heat interests. Each fought for space to lay tracks, sought public support for their lines, petitioned the city council for new franchises, and filed suits against the other. Mayor Livingston Mims was in the middle of the fray: he stood for "competition" but was accused of favoring the Atlanta elites with which both he and Hurt were identified. Atkinson represented "consolidation" of the trolley systems, and his side was represented in the 1901 city elections by the mayoral contender against Mims. The differences between the two parties escalated into heated debate in the newspapers, endless battles in the courts, and hotly contested elections. The matter was finally solved when a Boston syndicate, secretly representing Atkinson, bought out Hurt's interests. In 1902 all the electric and street railway facilities were consolidated under the Georgia Railway and Electric Company, the parent company of both the present-day Georgia Power Company and the Metropolitan Atlanta Rapid Transit Authority (MARTA).

A NEW CENTER FOR EDUCATION

There was no question about Atlanta's growth or its involvement in the latest urban technologies, such as the electric street railways, but there was some local concern as to how Atlanta was going to stay abreast of the latest in industry and enterprise, let alone culture and fashion. If Atlanta did not take care to educate its populace and to challenge its youth, it might lose what edge it had. The seat of Georgia's education was clearly the state university located in Athens, many miles from Atlanta, and a source of some jealous grumbling among the locals. Atlanta had nothing to compare to it, not for years after the Civil War.

In the decades after the Civil War Atlanta enjoyed numerous important developments in education, from kindergarten through the university level. Atlantans tended to treat education boosterishly, as a necessary component of urban progress, a handmaiden to commercial success, and a means to personal advancement. For black Atlantans, education meant racial uplift, a way out of economic depression, and a way up the social ladder. Whites regarded education for themselves similarly, but often considered education for blacks as a means to maintaining the racial status quo (i.e., African Americans should be educated to their place in the working classes, but not beyond). Ironically, two of the first universities in Atlanta were established for African Americans.

Today the Atlanta University Center comprises the largest consortium for black higher education in the world. Clark Atlanta University began as two separate entities, both in 1867, as northern missionaries established schools for the freed slaves. Clark began with the Summer Hill school for black children; Atlanta University, with classes in a boxcar in 1865, was granted its charter by the state

Atlanta University, as it appeared in the 1890s on its original campus, now Morris Brown College.

in 1867. Neither school restricted attendance by race, color, or sex. Clark University opened in 1877 and issued its first baccalaureate degree in 1883. Two other important schools followed: Morehouse College for men and Spelman College for women. Morehouse began as the Augusta Institute, moved to Atlanta in 1879 as the Atlanta Baptist Seminary, established its campus near Atlanta University, and changed its name to Morehouse College in 1913. Morehouse granted its first college degree in 1897. Spelman was founded in the basement of Friendship Baptist Church in 1883 as the Atlanta Baptist Female Seminary, and changed its name to honor the maternal family of John D. Rockefeller, a benefactor to the college. Spelman graduated its first class in 1887 and granted its first baccalaureate in 1901. Morris Brown College was chartered in 1885 by the African Methodist Episcopal Church for Christian and industrial work. These five schools plus the Interdenominational Theological Seminary constitute the Atlanta University Center today, which in the course of its century-long history has provided training for national leadership in black business, industry, culture, and politics.

Oglethorpe University was the first college for whites in Atlanta, a reinstitution of Oglethorpe College originally situated in Milledgeville. It opened its doors in 1870 with a high school, a college department, and a law department, and had plans for a medical college, a commercial department, and a civil engineering school, which were not developed. Oglethorpe held its first commencement the year after it opened. The school experimented with evening classes, thereby introducing the first night school in Atlanta.

In 1882, Nathaniel Harris of Bibb County introduced a resolution in the state legislature to establish a school of technology in Georgia. A committee was appointed in 1883 to study the matter. In 1885 the bill finally passed to establish the school as a branch of the University of Georgia, whose main campus, in Athens, was as old as the state itself. After no small promotional effort, Atlanta was selected as the site for the school, and in 1888 the

Marking the completion of the two main buildings at the new Georgia Institute of Technology in 1889.

Georgia Institute of Technology opened with 130 students, ten faculty members, and a course in mechanical engineering as its sole offering. In a few years, Georgia Tech began to offer degrees in electrical and civil engineering. With increased funding in the 1890s, Tech expanded its degrees, built its first dorms, and even offered a high school makeup track for underprepared students. Tech very quickly became the foundation of the white industrial, commercial, and political leadership in Atlanta.

White women were first offered collegiate education through Agnes Scott College in Decatur, Georgia. Founded by Reverend Frank H. Gaines, pastor of the Decatur Presbyterian Church, and George Washington Scott, a wealthy businessman, the school was named in honor of Scott's mother. Scott's gift of $100,000 was the largest ever given to a school at the time. Agnes Scott opened in 1889, priding itself on its curriculum: it was competitive with any of the prime northeastern colleges for men (or women!), except it had no industrial department. Agnes Scott was the first college in metropolitan Atlanta to be accredited by the Southern Association of Colleges and Secondary Schools, an acknowledgment of its superior training.

THE PUBLIC SCHOOLS

With Georgia Tech at home in Atlanta, with Agnes Scott nearby, and with a collection of growing black colleges (mostly ignored by the white community), Atlanta at last was a center for higher education. What was gained at the upper reaches of scholarship, though, had to be supported at the lower end—by the basics, the ABCs—but Atlanta's desire for public education was considerably less enthusiastic than its push for collegiate institutions. The city's school system was founded in 1872—late, by comparison to other major American cities—with eight grammar schools and two high schools, one for white girls and one for white boys. There was no high school for blacks and there were no kindergartens. Three of the grammar schools were for African Americans.

Dr. Daniel C. O'Keefe, a member of the city council, had introduced the resolution to establish public schools in 1871, whereupon the council appointed a board of education to carry out its preliminary directives. When the schools first opened only white teachers were used. The board preferred young, unmarried white women as teachers, who were terminated if they married; only when teachers were in short supply, as in the late 1880s, did the board hire married women. In 1874 two educated black men applied for teaching jobs and were denied employment; three years later two black women were hired. By this time the school board had learned of the advantages of using black teachers in the black schools; among other benefits their salaries were lower than those of whites.

The public school system was small, much smaller than the city's actual need for schools. The school board was cost-conscious to a fault. Their stringent economies kept them free of the political upheavals under the 1874 change in the charter, whereby the board of aldermen was created to watchdog every public expenditure; but for nearly two decades the Atlanta public schools were cited as having the lowest expenditures and receipts among systems in comparably sized cities.

The schools operated at capacity and never met the needs of the local populace. When the schools opened, only 2,800 pupils out of a possible 9,400 local children were enrolled. To meet tight budgets, the board of education shortened the school year, even charged tuition for a while. In 1887 the public schools went into double sessions; seventy pupils in a class was not an unusual number.

Corporal punishment was an issue for the public schools throughout the last decades of the nineteenth century. In 1897 a citizens' petition to the school board finally managed to get corporal punishment ended in the grammar schools, and from then on, physical punishment at Boys' High required parental approval to take place.

In the 1890s the first public kindergartens were introduced, but they received no funding from the city. The very first one was held at the home of Mrs. William Lawson Peel for one year, in 1880. Three more private kindergartens were added in other homes, and a more formal one was opened in 1888 at Washington Seminary for girls. The Atlanta Kindergarten School, under the auspices of the Atlanta Normal Training School (now Georgia State University), followed the teachings of Frederick Froebel, founder of the kindergarten idea; most of the trained teachers came from that school or the Capital Female College, a fashionable finishing school for girls. The Sheltering Arms Day Nursery Association had its beginnings in a mission on Marietta Street, and benefited from the support of teachers like Mrs. Eva Lovett, for whom Lovett school is named.

The activities around the 1895 Cotton States Exposition held in Atlanta gave rise to the Atlanta Free Kindergarten Association of 1896, which established a dozen kindergartens in town; it was the only women's association, among the many which lobbied for women's interests in the state capitol, to openly sign the lobbyist register, so popular was its cause. The Gate City Free Kindergarten Association, an outgrowth of the work of Gertrude Ware at Atlanta University, established kindergartens for African American children in the Fourth Ward, in south Atlanta, and on the west side. Kindergartens were the achievement of educated and purposeful white and black women. They conducted their kindergartens wherever large groups assembled for any length of time: at the Piedmont Chautauqua, at camp meetings and churches, at expositions and fairs, in private homes around the city, at charity locations such as the Methodist Children's Home in Decatur, and at the mills. Kindergartens were not publicly funded until they were incorporated into the city schools system in the twentieth century, nearly fifty years after they were first founded. (The State of Georgia remained without a statewide kindergarten program even longer.)

New Social Outlets

The increase in educational activities in Atlanta was accompanied by a correlative increase in all kinds of social activities—for personal enrichment, for spiritual uplift, for recreation, for welfare or charity, and for simple amusement. The amusements available

DARLENE ROTH AND ANDY AMBROSE / 81

to Atlantans in the late nineteenth century, in fact, were quite diverse, even if not so well developed as in some of the more affluent and larger urban centers of the Northeast. The DeGive Opera House was the city's primary auditorium, built in 1869 to seat two thousand people. The theater offered dramatic performances, public lectures, choral performances, operatic recitals, and the city's first can-can show (1875). Smaller concerts, dances, meetings, orations, and other entertainment were also held at the Concordia Hall, which seated five hundred and was primarily a German venue, as Hibernian Hall was an Irish one.

In 1880, Atlanta boasted only the amusement park at Ponce de Leon Springs, the fairgrounds at Oglethorpe Park, the landscaped flower beds and walks around city hall, and the bathing pool at Angiers Springs as public recreation areas. There were restorative springs in locations farther away, such as the spa at Lithia Springs, but they were not always within a reasonable distance for simple outings. The greenswards at Oakland Cemetery (established in 1850) and West View Cemetery (established in 1884) were also often used for outings and picnics. The grandest of all the green spaces was Ponce de Leon Springs, a "fashionable gathering place" located under what is now City Hall East. Opening in the 1870s, it boasted two springs, a lake for boating, cool shade, fresh air, rustic bridges, quaint walks, a bathhouse, and a refreshment stand. The springs were popular for picnics, barbecues, and Sunday afternoon concerts, and, eventually, baseball games.

Baseball had made its appearance in 1866 with a group of returning Civil War veterans calling themselves the Atlanta Baseball Club who played against a rival Atlanta team, Gate City Nine. The first game was played on May 18, 1866, with no grandstand, no popcorn, no peanuts, and no Coca-Cola; the teams battled for four hours nonstop until the last ball was hit. Final score: Atlanta 29, Gate City 127. Gate City took the game ball and gilded it.

Nearly twenty years later, in 1885, Henry Grady organized the Southern League, hoping baseball could be a symbol of Atlanta's progress and maturity. His Atlanta team never won anything but the trophy for having the largest opening crowds, and the Southern League collapsed in 1898. It was replaced by Abner

Powell's Southern Association, headquartered in Selma, Alabama.

Atlantans hated having an outsider own their team, and Powell was finally bought out in 1907 by a group headed by Walthal Joyner, Atlanta's fire chief and later mayor. Joyner was an avid fan: "I think I can do more good encouraging the home team to do some pennant winning than I can by sitting in my office at City Hall," he once boasted. Atlanta's team was more than sport; the Crackers—as they were called—were a walking advertisement for the city. A winning team meant a positive image; a losing team, a negative one. Well into the early 1900s, Atlanta bemoaned its team's record: "It is extremely unfortunate," complained the 1911 president of the Atlanta Chamber of Commerce, "that a city holding the position that Atlanta does in the South should be represented throughout this country by a tail-end team. The advertising that a city gets by supporting a winning team is of far more importance than is commonly supposed. A tail end team, on the other hand, casts a decided reflection on the city it represents." In those days winning baseball seasons were a thing of the future. Although there was a local African American team, the Atlanta Deppens, professional black baseball would not be seriously organized until World War I.

While many groups provided social outlets and benefits for their members, other groups organized themselves to extend welfare to needy members of their own racial, religious, gender, or ethnic groups. The City of Atlanta did not earmark municipal funds for public relief, a fact that induced the establishment of such benevolent groups, each with its own constituency. In 1858, the Hibernian Benevolent Society, still extant as the Hibernian Society, served less fortunate Irish; the Hebrew Benevolent Society, the Saint Andrew's Benevolent Society, the German Turnverein, and the Concordia Association (German and Jewish) were all active. Their black counterparts included the Sisters of Honor and the Brothers of Aid. In 1888, the city's chapter of the Benevolent and Protective Order of the Elks was founded, followed in 1890 by the arrival of the Salvation Army. Later in the 1890s, white charities included the Home for the Friendless, the Women's Christian Association Mission School,

The 1838 removal of the Cherokees, known as the Trail of Tears, symbolically depicted by contemporary artist Robert H. Annesley. (Courtesy of the artist.)

The Tullie Smith Farm House, on the grounds of the Atlanta History Center. The house dates from about 1845 and is one of few surviving antebellum structures in Atlanta.

The state flower, the Cherokee rose, drawn by eighteenth-century Georgia naturalist John Abbott. Abbott, who lived in Savannah, traveled through the state's interior drawing insects, small animals, and botanical specimens.

Solomon Luckie, a well-known African American barber in early Atlanta, licensed by the city to conduct his business in the Atlanta Hotel, was one of the civilians killed in the 1864 attack on the city during the Civil War.

A 1903 advertisement for Coca-Cola, the original product of Atlanta's premier corporation, founded in 1888 and now known the world over.

The intersection of Baker, Peachtree, and West Peachtree Streets in 1900. Now the site of Hardy Ivy Park, it has been transformed from outpost to fashionable suburb, to hotel row, to commercial district.

129—Wren's Nest, Home of Joel Chandler Harris
Atlanta. Ga.

The Wren's Nest, the home of newspaper reporter and early folklorist Joel Chandler Harris, whose Uncle Remus stories were drawn from African folktales.

BIRD'S-EYE VIEW OF THE COTTON STATES AND INTERNATIONAL EXPOSITION—ATLANTA, GA., U.S.A.
OPENS SEPTEMBER 18th. CLOSES DECEMBER 31st.
1895.

A bird's-eye view of the Cotton States and International Exposition, hosted by Atlanta in Piedmont Park in 1895. Today all that is left of the celebration are some stone steps and balustrades leading into the park.

Peachtree Street,
looking North from Viaduct,
Great White Way.

A 1920s postcard shows Peachtree Street looking north toward the Candler Building.

The commercial building boom, celebrated by the chamber of commerce magazine City Builder, *showing all of Atlanta's early skyscrapers.*

The Odd Fellows complex, a set of buildings on Auburn Avenue constructed between 1912 and 1915, featuring a drug store, an auditorium/movie theater, offices, retail space, and a roof garden nightclub.

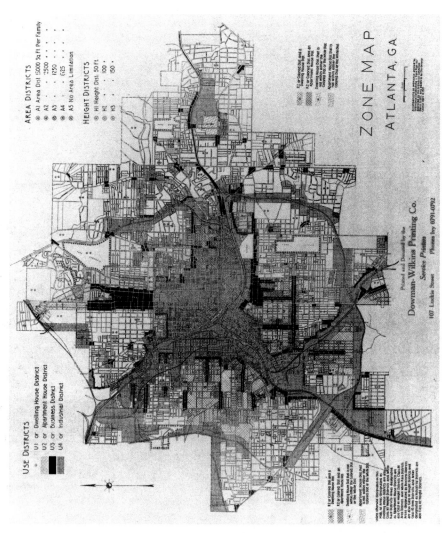

A 1922 zoning map of Atlanta, reserving sections of the city for "white," "colored," and "undetermined." The zoning ordinance that this map supported was later ruled unconstitutional.

The Edward Inmans, like many wealthy whites, built a new home in the developing suburbs of Buckhead in the early part of the twentieth century. Now known as the Swan House and located on the grounds of the Atlanta History Center, the Inman home is one of the city's finest classically inspired mansions.

VJ (Victory over Japan) Day in Atlanta, August 1945, signaled the end of World War II. Atlantans took to Peachtree Street to celebrate.

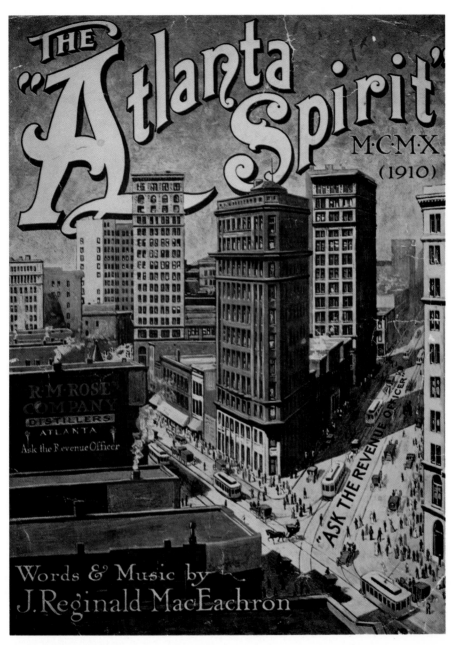

"The Atlanta Spirit"—here a play on words—a song celebrating Atlanta's famous boosterism and an ad for the R. M. Rose Company (later Four Roses), local distillers of alcoholic beverages.

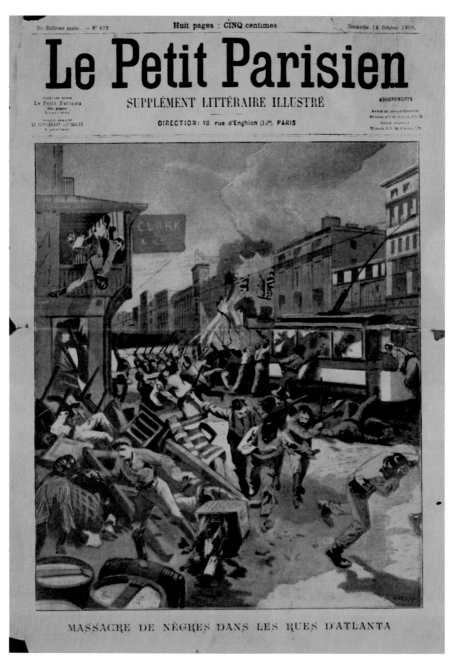

Dix-huitième année. — N° 922   Huit pages : CINQ centimes   Dimanche 14 Octobre 1906.

Le Petit Parisien

SUPPLÉMENT LITTÉRAIRE ILLUSTRÉ

DIRECTION: 13 rue d'Enghien (10ᵉ), PARIS

MASSACRE DE NÈGRES DANS LES RUES D'ATLANTA

The 1906 race riot made international headlines, as indicated by this French *magazine with the caption "Massacre of Negroes on Atlanta Streets." The loss of image was a shock for Atlanta.*

In the 1920s membership in the Ku Klux Klan was openly acknowledged; even the mayor was a member. Here a poster promotes Klan Day at the Southeastern Fair (located at Lakewood Fairgrounds).

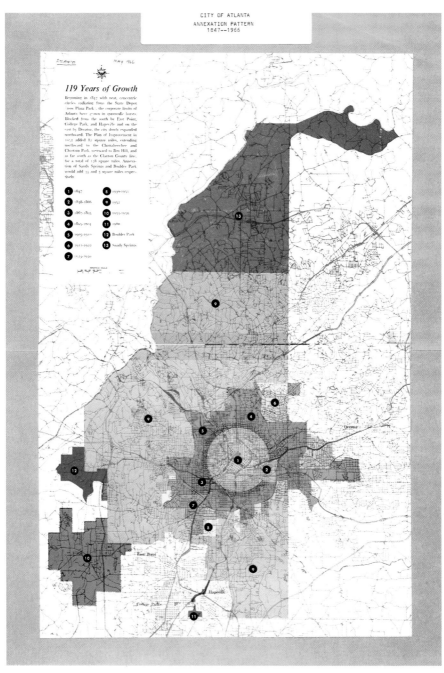

Proposed and actual city annexations. The 1952 Plan of Improvement (shown in pink) added 100,000 people to Atlanta and tripled the size of the city. The city limits have not expanded since, though suburban growth has continued.

" . . . the City of . . . Atlanta!" A moment of triumph as Atlantans, gathered at Underground, celebrate the announcement that the city has been chosen to host the 1996 Centennial Olympic Games.

Atlanta's Hartsfield International Airport, home of Delta Air Lines, is now the city's transportation link to the world. (Courtesy Delta Air Lines)

The Carter Presidential Center, including the Carter Library and the offices of former U.S. president Jimmy Carter, supports international work in health, political arbitration, and economic development.

Inside the Piedmont Driving Club, founded in 1887, as it looked in 1910. The "driving club" was the most elite social organization in the city.

the Sheltering Arms nursery, and—for blacks—the Carrie Steele Logan Orphanage, founded in 1890.

Cultural activity expanded on all fronts. The Capital City Club (1883) and the Piedmont Driving Club (1887) were indications that the business elite was becoming group-minded, even "clubby." Atlanta's social scene was anything but orderly; southerners who were accustomed to obtaining success through family ties were put off by the capitalistic entrepreneurs who obtained success by making money. Yet Atlanta was open to all of them in business and to most of them in their clubs—the entrepreneurs, the merely civic-minded, and those with enough chutzpah to enter the sacrosanct quarters of the elite associations on their own terms. In such a din of class reorganization, Atlanta differed from the more stagnant southern towns that adhered to the old social standards—Charleston, Mobile, Savannah. There outsiders were not welcomed into the leadership of the city. Period.

Atlanta's women took the lead in club activities, often being the first to organize in the state for education and culture, promoting

Mrs. Marion Jackson and Florence King Jackson, two fashionable Atlantans about to take a drive, outside the home of Captain Henry Jackson on Capitol Avenue. They and their carriage are dressed for a wedding or other celebration.

one civic cause after another, taking on unpopular issues and some elements of controversy. Both black and white women, as seen in their philanthropic activities, became very active in the formation of cultural organizations to serve needs in the community. The first organizations of any size and impact among white women were the patriotic lineage groups, the "daughters" clubs. Atlanta founded the country's second oldest chapter of the Daughters of the American Revolution (1890), and it formed one of the first chapters of the United Daughters of the Confederacy (1895). The Georgia Federation of Women's Clubs and its largest member group, the Atlanta Woman's Club (for whites only), were founded in the mid-1890s. The Atlanta Federation of Negro Women's Clubs was founded about the same time. Sororities, literary societies, chautauquas (self-improvement groups), social clubs, kindergartens, mothers clubs—all abounded among the women of both races. Some Atlanta women, such as Nellie Peters Black and Selena Sloan Butler, were nationally recognized for their leadership in women's club activities. Besides kindergartens and parent-teacher associations, the women concerned themselves with the improvement of schools (for children in Atlanta and in rural Georgia), the provision of police matron, for female inmates in statewide jails, humane assistance for young female workers, compulsory and equal education for women and girls, free libraries, age of consent laws, feminine hygiene, and—last and also least—the Woman Suffrage Movement.

THE RISE OF SEGREGATION AND THE MAKING OF BLACK ATLANTA

The Woman Suffrage Movement, as it played itself out in the South, was a shadow of a complex world—a world split along gender and racial lines. Atlanta women—white women, that

Members of the Atlanta Equal Suffrage Association parading in 1913 for the right of women to vote. The city granted women the right to vote in local elections in 1919, just months before the Nineteenth Amendment to the Constitution granted universal suffrage. Atlanta was the only municipality in Georgia to be so progressive.

is—began in 1894 to campaign for the right to vote and to be represented in the democratic process. The Atlanta Equal Suffrage Association, as progressive as it was, was a latecomer to the ranks of the national movement and marched under a prejudicial banner: as a southern organization, it proclaimed that if white women could have the vote, they could neutralize the votes of black men. These suffrage efforts were but one reflection of the growing separation of the races, an open, relentless, and later violent separation, as two entirely different cities evolved.

A black world emerged in the decades following the Civil War, a kind of secret city that was unknown to the white populace. It was pulled into being by rising common interests and pushed into being by segregation and legal restrictions on black enterprise, political power, and social interaction. The longer slavery was over, the more numerous and picky the restrictions became. In a paradox of daily living, segregation took away black freedom as it gave blacks the opportunity, and the need, to become autonomous. African Americans were drawn to the city because of the advantages it seemed to offer over the countryside; once in Atlanta they congregated in increasingly segregated neighborhoods in the inner city. By 1890 the majority of Atlantans lived in either all-white or all-black neighborhoods, a separation that had not existed before the war. The strongest black enclaves clustered in the Old Fourth Ward, where Morris Brown was originally located, and on the south side, where Clark University was originally located. And a growing concentration appeared in proximity to the other African American colleges on the west side. Where Spelman College took over the old MacPherson Barracks (which had been abandoned in favor of a new location, present-day Fort MacPherson), there was room to grow. Where Atlanta University built its first facilities, there was a place for faculty homes, and house lots for respectable citizens who could afford to buy a sizable plot of land.

A few African Americans accumulated real estate, but more of them had to put what money they had in to personal property—

clothing, furniture, and other possessions. The small landed black upper class perched precariously on top of a large working-class black population in Atlanta; by 1870, 311 of them owned property out of a population of 9,000. These few hundred enjoyed education and prosperity on a par with white citizens, but not white political power or economic clout. One of these privileged blacks was Alonzo Herndon. Born into slavery in Social Circle, Georgia, he rose to become Atlanta's first black millionaire. His success stemmed from several sources: an insurance company, a string of barbershops, shrewd real estate developments, and banking investments. His home near the Morris Brown College campus is still a showplace for tastes that were in vogue at the turn of the century.

Racial relations were often strained, but few incidents of violence were reported in Atlanta between the end of the Civil War and the end of the century. The Ku Klux Klan existed in the city, though publicly its existence was often denied. The Klan had stronger operations in the country than it did in Atlanta. Once, in 1879, a handful of Klansmen rode through several Atlanta neighborhoods; their skirmish threatened—but did not harm— any African American citizens. A more serious altercation had occurred some years earlier between Atlanta blacks and the Federal soldiers stationed at the old MacPherson Barracks over the beating of shoemaker Festus Flipper. Order was restored, but not before two hundred residents near the Barracks had armed themselves.

Residential segregation was increasing along with the restrictive ordinances affecting shopping and travel. The practices of Jim Crow—legislated segregation and legalized discrimination—were emerging as a means for racial control. The streetcars were segregated: a smoking area in the rear accommodated blacks, who had to enter from the rear, while whites entered from the front of the cars. The same process held on southern trains, each of which carried separate cars for black and white passengers. A ladies car carried white women and children—with their attending servants—and nonsmoking white men; a smoking car carried white men and those black men who preferred tobacco smoke to the segregated compartment. All other black passengers rode in the separate car reserved for them. Northern trains passing through the South would add a car for the black passengers. Waiting rooms were segregated as well, offering less comfort and convenience for black travelers than for white ones.

ATLANTA'S EXPOSITIONS

In 1881 an important event occurred that signaled a new direction in Atlanta's economic and social history. Atlanta hosted the first of several "international" expositions with the objective of increasing outside investments and attention to itself. Two more expositions followed in 1887 and 1895, and these promotional events put Atlanta's best foot forward and remain among some of Atlanta's most memorable historic moments.

The first exposition signaled a new emphasis in Atlanta's social and economic history. The city wanted to boost itself into larger markets, draw outside investments, and promote its image in an increasingly attentive international press. Promoter/entrepreneur Hannibal Kimball headed the planning committee for the International Cotton Exposition of 1881, which drew 350,000 people to it from thirty-three states and seven foreign countries. At the end of the exposition, the buildings were converted into a textile mill that began operations in 1882.

In 1887 Atlanta hosted the Piedmont Exposition at Henry Grady's instigation. Though not national in scope, it did keep Atlanta in the limelight and counter the impression that Prohibition (passed locally the same year) had curtailed business initiatives. The high point of the fair was President Grover Cleveland's visit on October 18.

In 1895, Atlanta hosted the granddaddy of all the local fairs, the Cotton States and International Exposition. Envisioned on a par with the Chicago Columbian Exposition held just two years prior, this exposition was actually barely one-fourth the size of its northern predecessor. It and the two smaller expos that preceded it were intended to be regional responses to be a national celebratory trend. In this vein, Atlanta hosted the president (Grover Cleveland again), displayed the Liberty Bell, and commissioned John Philip Sousa to write a special march for the occasion. Piedmont Park, site of the exposition, was transformed into a magic land of midways, lakes, exhibition halls, entertainment and refreshment stands, decorations, electric lights, and special performers from circuses and vaudeville circuits.

The Cotton States and International Exposition, even more than to advertise Atlanta, was to benefit the southern economy and help reinstate the South as a full partner in the national marketplace. In this, Atlanta took the lead, grabbed the spotlight, and promoted its centrality to the region as the demonstrable heart of the New South. Though it was not a financial success (several local businessmen had to bail out the exposition at the end), the 1895 fair

The Woman's Building at the 1895 Exposition. While the other buildings were built in a clean, "modern," industrial style, the Woman's Building with its beaux arts architecture evoked a more classical, ornamental, "feminine" expression.

was the most successful advertisement of its day: thirteen thousand a day came to the fair; one million visitors in all. It received national and some international press, most of it very laudatory. There were buildings devoted to minerals, agriculture, forestry, manufacturing, railroads, transportation, and electricity, all filled with southern products, resources, inventions, and accomplishments.

Most popular among the buildings were the Woman's Building and the Negro Building. The Woman's Building modeled itself on the Woman's Building in Chicago, showcasing the "New Woman," who, in the words of Emma Mims Thompson, president of the Board of Women Managers, was "neither the antagonist nor the rival of man, but his co-worker and helpmeet." The Woman's Building was designed by Elise Mercur of Pittsburgh, Pennsylvania, in classical style, and housed an assembly room for daily conferences, a model school, a day nursery and kindergarten, exhibits, paintings, and a model kitchen. The exhibits came from all over the nation and included everything from canned goods to painted china and other handiwork. A library contained books written by women, and a hall of inventions included a portable bathtub, a bedclothes fastener, a marble shooting toy, an exercise machine, and a snow plow. The daily conventions were an important aspect of the Woman's Building; women from all over the country sat in congresses for a wide variety of organizations. Several Atlanta women's organizations trace their origins to congresses at the 1895 Exposition—the Atlanta chapters of the National Association of Colored Women, the National Council of Jewish Women, and the Atlanta Federation of Woman's Clubs.

The Negro Building was completely unprecedented in world's fairs. Designed, managed, outfitted, and built by African Americans, the building was a 270-foot-long wood frame and concrete hall with towers and flags and symbolic black figures. The exhibitions inside constituted the first major southern exhibit on black achievement in national history: they spotlighted the progress of the race since the end of slavery, African American success in the midst of increasing segre-

Inside the Negro Building at the Cotton States and International Exposition of 1895. Among the exhibits was a statue of a slave breaking his shackles; to the left of him was an oil portrait of Frederick Douglass. Douglass died that year and was replaced by Booker T. Washington as the leading African American of the day.

gation, and hopes for a better future. The U.S. Congress had donated $20,000 of federal money toward the exposition with the stipulation that such a building be created, and now national journalists were far more interested in its story than in the industries of the South.

The opening day ceremonies were impressive, including parades and many speeches. Horse-drawn carriages carried the notables, politicians, and honored guests to Piedmont Park, where the exposition took place. As a representative of the Negro community, Booker T. Washington, the most widely recognized black educator in the country, was allowed to address the opening crowds. He admonished both blacks and whites to "cast down your buckets where you are . . . by making friends in every manly way of the people of all races by whom we are surrounded." Other of his words were more conciliatory and seemed to condone segregation: "In all things purely social," he said, "we can be as separate as the fingers, yet as the hand in all things essential to mutual progress." He had been introduced by Governor Rufus Bullock, who shook his hand at the conclusion of his remarks—a "moral revolution," the *Atlanta Constitution* pronounced the occasion; "Compromise!" pronounced his critics.

On the heels of Washington's speech, Atlanta University called for a conference on the conditions of the Negro in all American cities. The conference became annual, headed up by William Edward Burghardt Du Bois, who arrived in Atlanta to teach at Atlanta University in 1897. Du Bois, one of the greatest scholars of his day of any race, spent about a third of his lifetime in Atlanta. Aloof, intellectual, reserved, fastidious, and difficult, Du Bois was a brilliant teacher and thinker who spearheaded racial investigations and commentary that are still classic studies today and were the only ones of their kind at the turn of the century. His approach to racial matters differed significantly from Booker T. Washington's, creating a dichotomy of opinions that sparked controversies and debates that continue even today.

VISIONS OF THE FUTURE

The 1895 Exposition created enduring images of a New South—industrialized, modern, progressive politically and economically, a place where men of every rank could find work and women might find new roles. It also created enduring images of a not-so-new South, one that was racially unbalanced, one that was infinitely dedicated to the cultivation of cotton and to economic influence from the outside. The visions of the future that the Exposition posited were as complicated as they were contradictory, as conservative as they were urbane, and, for Atlantans, as optimistic as ever.

The theme of the future was picked up by Atlanta newspapers at the end of the century, where advertisements, editorials, and articles were full of predictions and queries: When does the new century actually begin, 1900 or 1901? What would the city next accomplish? Would H. M. Atkinson ever finish the trolley system? Would Atlanta get a new depot and at long last end the congestion in the heart of the city? How many more skyscrapers would go up? Would the success and prosperity of the last year continue? How many more people would settle in the city? Would international events overwhelm the country? Would the problem of the new century be, as W.E.B. Du Bois predicted, the "problem of the color line"?

Journalists indulged themselves in speculations, in depictions of holiday celebrations, and in taking potshots at the city's politicians. Among the lengthy articles in the *Atlanta Constitution* was one describing the latest inventions: an electric exercising machine, a new can opener, audible buoys, a bathtub hot-water heater, a combination screwdriver/holder, a legless wheelbarrow, and a trunk that turned into a desk. A new combination world globe and clock could tick away the hours, minutes, and seconds and reveal the world's hot spots at the same time. Not all the gadgets were useful and not all the predictions were optimistic, as the editor poetically but gloomily concluded: "If prophets are to be relied upon then the twentieth century will be a crimson one, and will bear witness to changes as great as they are unexpected. War now almost encircles the globe, . . . while Mars rides down the morning of a new century about to burst upon a world which glories only in new things."

Atlanta
The Commercial City, 1900–1940

Office buildings are to Atlanta what furniture is to Grand Rapids and automobiles are to Detroit.

—Charles Palmer, President, Association of Office Builders and Managers, 1930

The "Atlanta Spirit"

uring the Cotton States and International Exposition of 1895, Atlanta had announced to the world its aspiration to become a "New South" city whose diversified and prosperous economy would anchor and set the example for a changing South. As the first four decades of the new century unfolded, Atlanta achieved many of its objectives. The city's population grew dramatically, its economy became more diverse and vibrant, and its cultural and educational institutions matured and increased in number. This rapid growth and development was undercut and slowed somewhat by the severe economic depression that settled upon the nation in the 1930s. Nonetheless, by 1940 Atlanta had emerged as one of the preeminent urban centers of the South.

The growth and expansion that would characterize much of this era were apparent everywhere in early twentieth-century Atlanta. The city's population, which stood at 89,000 in 1900, tripled during the next three decades. The physical size and dimensions of Atlanta also grew as the city added communities like Edgewood, Kirkwood, and West End to its boundaries and miles to its circumference. Beyond the city limits, new suburban developments arose, made possible by the presence of the streetcar and later the automobile. Even Atlanta's skyline began to expand with the addition of the city's earliest "skyscrapers"—the Equitable Building, the Flatiron Building, the Empire Building, and the Candler Building. And in between these skyscrapers—most of which operated as office buildings—emerged a whole host of commercial structures (like the Peachtree arcade and the Muse's and Davison-Paxon department stores), hotels (such as the Piedmont, the Georgian Terrace, the Ansley, and the Winecoff), and new government buildings (a city auditorium, a post office and federal courthouse, a new Fulton County courthouse, and a new million-dollar city hall).

Atlanta's explosive growth was regarded by most city boosters as a positive development, one that should be promoted and encouraged. Louie Newton, editor of the *City Builder* magazine, for example, lauded what he termed the "Atlanta

Spirit"—the pervasive belief that whatever was good for business was good for Atlanta and that what was good for Atlanta
was good for all of its citizens. Thus, in the name of business
and progress, the city's early twentieth-century boosters
encouraged not only commercial growth, but also the development of a myriad of cultural, artistic, and sports activities
and institutions that they hoped would transform Atlanta into
an urban center of regional and national prominence. In the
process of promoting and implementing these changes, Atlanta
was remade and its economic, cultural, and physical structure
dramatically altered.

THE GROWTH OF COMMERCE

Atlanta's early twentieth-century growth and expansion was
based in part on the development of a new economic orientation
for the city. In the nineteenth century, the city's vital railroad connections had helped transform Atlanta into a rail and distribution center for the Southeast. The railroad industry's impact on
and dominance of the local economy during this period was
reflected not only in the number of railroad-related industries
found in Atlanta, but also in the physical positioning of the city
around the railways. The center or heart of Atlanta lay at the
convergence of its railroad lines, and Atlanta's primary businesses were concentrated along its tracks. The turn of the century,
however, witnessed a gradual realignment of the city's economy
and its relationship to the railroads. The rail transportation
industry remained the city's largest employer until the 1920s, but
increasingly Atlanta's economic and physical expansion was
spurred not by the railroads but by commercial growth. The
emergence in the early twentieth century of a new business corridor that stretched northward along Peachtree Street away from
Five Points (and the railway hub that had earlier marked the economic and physical center of Atlanta) and the construction
(beginning in the 1920s) of a series of viaducts that elevated the
city above the tracks symbolically signaled the end of the rail-

road's dominance of the local economy and the rise of a more diversified economic order centered around commerce.

FORWARD ATLANTA

A 1920s chamber of commerce–styled welcome to Atlanta, part of a larger campaign to bring not only people but businesses to the city.

Atlanta's business and civic leaders were well aware of the economic changes taking place in the city during the first decades of the twentieth century, and city hall and the chamber of commerce joined together to vigorously promote the growth of commerce. The most ambitious and successful of these promotional efforts began in 1925 when W.R.C. Smith and Ivan Allen, Sr., of the Atlanta Chamber of Commerce launched an aggressive national advertising campaign entitled "Forward Atlanta" that was designed to lure new businesses to the city. The campaign proved to be a phenomenal success. Some 762 new businesses moved to Atlanta between 1925 and 1929, bringing tens of thousands of jobs and adding an estimated $34 million in annual payrolls to the city's economy. Included among the businesses that made Atlanta their regional headquarters during this period were such corporate giants as the Davison-Paxon department store (later merged with Macy's); Sears-Roebuck, which built its southeastern retail and mail-order headquarters on Ponce de Leon Avenue; and General Motors, which established a manufacturing plant at Lakewood in 1928.

The success of the Forward Atlanta campaign reshaped the city's economy and put it in better shape to weather the gathering storms of a national economic depression. It also completed Atlanta's transformation into a city of commerce. By 1930, Atlanta was only the twenty-ninth largest city in the United States, but it ranked second in terms of available office space. In addition to office buildings, early twentieth-century Atlanta also contained a widening array of commercial structures concentrated in the Fairlie-Poplar area of downtown and a large number of theaters and hotels in the entertainment district known as the "Great White Way."

THE BLACK SIDE: SWEET AUBURN

To the east of Fairlie-Poplar and the "Great White Way" was Auburn Avenue, a separate business/entertainment district reserved for Atlanta's nonwhite residents. As late as the turn of the century, many African American entrepreneurs in Atlanta were still locating their businesses next door to those of white businessmen and had even provided services to an exclusively white clientele. Alonzo Herndon, a former slave and the founder of Atlanta Life Insurance Company, for example, owned a very successful barbershop located on Peachtree Street whose clients were white and included some of the wealthiest and most powerful business and civic leaders in the city. With the rise, however, of Jim Crow segregation and the violence and destruction occasioned by the 1906 race riot (discussed elsewhere in this chapter), black-owned and -operated businesses in Atlanta

White business leaders meet in 1930 to celebrate the building of the Third National Bank Building, one of the skyscrapers built in the early decades of the twentieth century.

increasingly restricted their services to the African American community and their addresses to Auburn Avenue.

The construction of new buildings along Auburn Avenue during the early part of the twentieth century provided much-needed office space for the increasing number and diversity of black professionals, businesses, and trade and service organizations that were moving to the city. The Odd Fellows Building, built in 1912–15, housed a drugstore, an auditorium, offices for black professionals and entrepreneurs, and a rooftop garden where dances and receptions were held. Other important office buildings and multiuse structures constructed on Auburn Avenue during this period include the Rucker Building (built in 1904 by Henry A. Rucker, the first African American collector of internal revenue in Georgia) and the Herndon Building (built in 1924 by Alonzo Herndon). By 1920 there were already 72 black-owned businesses and 20 black professionals located on the avenue; ten years later that number had climbed to 121 businesses and 39 professionals. Included in this mix were insurance companies

The Atlanta Mutual Leadership Club in front of the Odd Fellows Building on Auburn Avenue, c. 1920. Alonzo Herndon, founder of the Atlanta Life Insurance Company, is the center of the photo.

such as Standard Life Insurance and Atlanta Life Insurance Company (one of the largest black-owned companies in the nation); stores; banks and lending institutions, such as Citizens Trust Bank and Mutual Federal; entertainment centers; hotels; restaurants; beauty schools; funeral homes; and newspapers, including the *Atlanta Independent* and later the *Atlanta Daily World*. Also grouped along the avenue were many of the city's largest and best-known black churches, like Big Bethel A.M.E., Wheat Street Baptist, and Ebenezer Baptist (where Martin Luther King, Jr., his father, and his grandfather served as pastors).

As this brief listing suggests, "Sweet Auburn" (as John Wesley Dobbs, grandmaster of the Prince Hall Masons, dubbed the street in the 1930s) provided Atlanta's African American community with many of the services, jobs, and funds denied them elsewhere in the city as a result of racial discrimination and segregation. And as Sweet Auburn continued to grow and prosper during the first half of the twentieth century, it also gained in regional stature and influence. "Auburn [Avenue] is not just a street," the *Atlanta Independent* observed in 1926. "It is an institution with influence and power not only among Georgians but American Negroes everywhere. It is the heart of Negro big business, a result of Negro cooperation and evidence of Negro possibility."

Jim Crow restrictions and regulations in Atlanta, as elsewhere in the early twentieth-century South, increasingly separated the city's black and white populations. African Americans in Atlanta patronized their own separate business/entertainment districts, attended their own separate schools and churches, and resided in their own separate communities. In 1932, African American business leaders also established their own separate chamber of commerce to promote black commercial growth and development within the city. (Ironically, although the Atlanta Chamber of Commerce and the Negro Chamber of Commerce never merged during this period, both remained members of the same national chamber of commerce.) Thus while black and white business leaders in Atlanta operated in different sectors of the city and engaged in separate promotional efforts, both groups contributed to the growth of a more diversified local economy and the transformation of Atlanta during the early twentieth century from a regional transportation center into a center of commerce.

ARTS AND ENTERTAINMENT

"HIGH" CULTURE — Commercial growth and expansion were not the only goals of the city's early twentieth-century boosters. In their push to make Atlanta a city on a par with other national urban centers, Atlanta's civic and business leaders also stressed the need to develop a wide range of cultural, artistic, and recreational organizations and activities. The effort was not a new one. Atlanta had hosted opera singers, musicals, plays, and symphonies during the nineteenth century and had even constructed elegant settings in which to view these performances (such as the 1,600-seat Davis Hall, built in 1866, and the DeGive Opera House, constructed in 1870). In the early twentieth century these efforts continued and resulted in an Atlanta performance by the Metropolitan Opera

Company of New York in 1901 and again in 1905. Unfortunately, these local performances were not well attended.

By 1909, however, a critical moment for cultural development had arrived. Civic leaders and music lovers were anxious to show off the city's new auditorium-armory (which had cost $250,000 to construct) and to announce Atlanta's arrival as a center of culture and refinement in the South. Accordingly, the city organized a "Great Southern Music Festival," which brought the Dresden Philharmonic Orchestra and Metropolitan Opera star Geraldine Ferrar to Atlanta to perform. The success of this endeavor prompted local sponsorship of the Met, and, beginning in 1910, the opera company began traveling to Atlanta for an annual spring performance—an arrangement that would last, with occasional interruption, until 1986. (An early highlight of this annual series was the performance in 1910 of world-famous tenor Enrico Caruso as Radames in *Aida*.)

Other local organizations, like the Atlanta Music Club (established in 1916), brought additional nationally known musical entertainers and symphonies to the city during this period and

Enrico Caruso played Samson in a 1915 Metropolitan Opera production of Samson and Delilah *at the height of the first "Met Week" in Atlanta.*

promoted as well the development of Atlanta's own symphony orchestra. Also emerging during the first decades of the twentieth century were a number of civic and cultural organizations, including the Atlanta Art Association (chartered in 1905), to which Mrs. Joseph High later gave her home (and her name) for an art museum; the Atlanta Writers Club (organized in 1914); and the Atlanta Historical Society (founded in 1926).

POPULAR MUSIC — Classical music and "high" culture and art were not the only forms of entertainment available in Atlanta during this era. In the 1920s, the city also became a recording center for blues and country music, and musicians from across the South traveled to Atlanta to perform and to record. Blues singers such as Blind Willie McTell, Buddy Moss, and "Barbecue Bob" Hicks not only played in area clubs, taverns, and homes, but also recorded their songs in local studios set up by Columbia and Decca Records. Atlanta was a regional recording and performance center for country music as well during this period. Companies such as Okeh and Columbia Records sent represen-

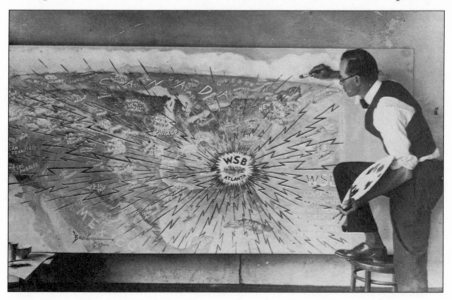

WSB, *the South's first radio station, began broadcasting in 1922. The broadcast area was not quite as large as that shown in the photo.*

tatives to the city to capture the musical offerings of early country stars like Fiddling John Carson and Gid Tanner and the Skillet Lickers, who performed at local fiddling contests or square dances. Those Atlantans who were not able to see these country musicians live or to buy their records had the opportunity to listen to them on the South's first radio station, WSB, which began broadcasting in Atlanta in 1922.

Atlanta audiences could also take in concerts and performances from some of the nation's best-known musicians and "big" bands during this era. Vocalists like Rudy Vallee and band leaders Tommy Dorsey and Benny Goodman included Atlanta on their concert tours. Blues singers Bessie Smith, Ethel Waters, and Ma Rainey also traveled to Atlanta to sing, most frequently at the black-owned and operated 81 Theatre on Decatur Street or the Top Hat Club on Auburn Avenue. Other well-known black musicians, including Count Basie, Duke Ellington, and Cab Calloway, were initially reluctant to travel to the South because of Jim Crow restrictions, but beginning in the mid-1930s these performers also began to appear in local nightclubs, theaters, and auditoriums.

While the musical appeal of the diverse group of artists who performed and recorded in Atlanta during the 1920s and 1930s crossed racial lines, the audiences that came to hear these musicians and the sites in which they performed remained strictly segregated. Black Atlantans, for example, were not allowed to attend the performances of the Metropolitan Opera; they organized instead their own classical concerts and offerings held in area churches or on the campuses of the Atlanta University Center schools. At other times, when both white and black audiences came to hear a musical performance, racial segregation was maintained in a variety of ways. Artists who performed at the Top Hat on Auburn Avenue, for example, played throughout the week to black audiences. On Saturday night, however, the establishment was reserved for whites. On another occasion, when both black and white Atlantans were invited to a classical musical concert sponsored by the Commission on Interracial Cooperation, the audience was split down the middle, with

African Americans on one side and whites on the other. The most common segregation pattern for racially mixed Atlanta audiences, however, was to restrict African Americans to the balcony

An undated performance of Heaven Bound, *at Big Bethel African Methodist Episcopal Church. This unique and long-lived morality play was first performed in 1930.*

(or "buzzard roost," as it became known). At the Fox Theatre, for example, black patrons had to enter the building through a long flight of stairs on the outside of the building to reach their seats in the balcony. When racially mixed audiences attended the performances of black musicians and bands at the Municipal Auditorium, however, the pattern was somewhat reversed: whites were in the stands and African Americans were on the floor where they could dance if they wished.

DANCING — As the preceding example suggests, southern racial etiquette of the times did not permit African Americans and whites to mix on the dance floor—largely because of white concerns that such associations might encourage thoughts of physical intimacy and social equality. Therefore, segregation prevailed in the city's clubs and dance halls during this era. Black Atlantans were barred from white dance halls and attended instead dances held at the rooftop garden of the Odd Fellows Building, the Top Hat Club, the Sunset Casino, or a number of other nightclub spots located in the city's black communities. White Atlantans similarly patronized white establishments.

With the growth of elite private social clubs such as the Piedmont Driving Club, the Capital City Club, and the Brookhaven, Druid Hills, and East Lake Country Clubs, the Atlanta dance scene became even further segregated by class and religious background. Membership in these clubs was restricted to the wealthiest and most influential of Atlanta's elite white society and remained closed not only to African Americans but to Jews as well. Atlanta's Jewish community responded to this slight by establishing its own private social clubs—the Standard, the Mayfair, and the Progressive.

MOVING PICTURES — Moving pictures, which had first appeared in Atlanta during the 1895 Cotton States and International Exposition, became an increasingly popular diversion in the early twentieth century. By 1914, it was estimated that between twenty-five and thirty thousand white Atlantans were attending the city's movie theaters every day. (No comparable figures are available for black theatergoers, but the largest movie houses in the city at the time admitted African Americans—though they were strictly segregated and largely confined to the balcony—and a number of black movie theaters were also found along Decatur Street.) Movie houses also quickly expanded in number and location throughout the city and came to include such palatial and elegant settings as the Howard Theater (built in 1920), the Fox Theatre (which opened to the public in 1929), and the Loew's Grand (originally the DeGive Opera House).

A number of key film events occurred in the city during this era, such as the 1915 showing of *Birth of a Nation* (discussed further below), which was viewed by over a fourth of Atlanta's white population. The opening of the "Fabulous Fox" in 1929 was another of these key events. The Fox Theatre, an architectural landmark of the era, was conceived, designed, and constructed through the efforts of the Yaarab Temple of Atlanta (a

Atlanta's "Fabulous Fox" Theatre, completed in 1929 by the Yaarab Shrine Temple. The Fox, now a multipurpose auditorium, is Atlanta's oldest and most elegant movie house.

Shriner organization) and featured storefront space, a banquet hall and ballroom, and kitchen facilities. The crowning achievement of the complex was the auditorium, or theater, with its combined Egyptian and Middle Eastern decorative motifs, tented balconies, simulated "starlit" sky, remarkable acoustics, and 3,610-pipe Möller organ, which could be raised to stage level or lowered out of sight.

Although the Yaarab Temple ran into financial difficulties before the theater was completed, a leasing agreement worked out between the Yaarab Temple and Fox Theatres Corporation of New York allowed the theater to open to the public on Christmas Day 1929—only two months after the stock market crash that signaled the beginning of the Great Depression. The Depression was nowhere in evidence on opening day, however, as crowds lined up around the block in the cold, drizzling rain to buy tickets (priced between 15 and 75 cents) for the afternoon's entertainment. Included in the opening day's presentations were a community sing-along featuring the "Mighty" Möller organ; a performance by the Fox Grand Orchestra, under the directorship of Enrico Leide; a program of dancing girls (Fanchon and Marco's "Sunkist Beauties"); a showing of *Steamboat Willie*, a proto–Mickey Mouse cartoon; Fox Movietone News; and the feature film *Salute*, a West Point romance starring George O'Brien, Helen Chandler, and Stepin Fetchit.

As exciting as this opening event was, an even grander moment in Atlanta's motion picture history occurred almost exactly ten years later when the movie *Gone with the Wind* had its world premiere in Atlanta. The movie was based upon the novel of the same name, written by Atlanta native Margaret Mitchell. Mitchell's novel had proved to be a phenomenal success when it was published in 1936, selling more than a million copies in the first six months and garnering a Pulitzer Prize the following year. Encouraged by the book's success, film producer David O. Selznick paid $50,000—then a record—for the movie rights to the novel.

While the film was being produced, rumors circulated that the premiere might occur in New York City, but Atlanta, home of

The Ebenezer Baptist Church choir performing at the Junior League ball during the premiere of Gone with the Wind, *1939. Martin Luther King, Jr., is among the children in slave dress at the center of the photo.*

the book's author and site of many of the novel's scenes, won out in the end. On December 14, 1939, the festivities began with a Peachtree Street parade and ended later that evening with a series of parties, including a *Gone with the Wind* ball at the Municipal Auditorium sponsored by the city's Junior League. Performing at the ball were the Ebenezer Baptist Church choir (which included a youthful Martin Luther King, Jr.) and the orchestras of Kay Kyser and Enrico Leide. Portions of the evening's performances were broadcast nationally over the NBC radio network.

The movie's world premiere the following evening focused even more national and international attention on Atlanta. More than two thousand notables, including the book's author, stars of the film and other Hollywood celebrities, local politicians, civic leaders, and governors of five southern states attended the event,

The gala Gone with the Wind *premiere at the Loew's Grand Theatre on Peachtree Street, December 15, 1939.*

which was held at the Loew's Grand. The theater's original facade had been altered to resemble a Greek Revival plantation house, and a huge medallion, featuring the likenesses of Rhett Butler (played in the movie by Clark Gable) and Scarlett O'Hara (Vivien Leigh), hung above the pediment. Movietone News and Pathé film crews, as well as representatives from newspapers, magazines, and radio stations all over the country, were present in Atlanta that night to capture the moment for their audiences back home.

Gone with the Wind soon proved to be as phenomenal a success as a film as it had been as a book. The movie grossed $14 million in its first year of distribution and won ten Academy Awards in 1939, including best picture, best actress (Vivien Leigh), and best supporting actress (Hattie McDaniel as Mammy). Ironically, McDaniel, the first African American to receive an Oscar, had not been present at the movie's premiere in Atlanta. David Selznick, fearing that white southerners would resent the presence of Hattie McDaniel and the film's other black actors, had forbidden them all from attending the event. His fears, however, appear to have been misplaced. Most southern whites found little to object to in McDaniel's portrayal of Mammy, and although both she and the film received harsh criticism from some organizations like the National Association for the Advancement of Colored People for the film's depiction of African Americans, other individuals and groups (including the Atlanta Ladies Memorial Association) were quick to praise the authenticity of McDaniel's performance.

In the years following its release, *Gone with the Wind* continued to be an enormously popular film, both in America and abroad. By 1989, the fiftieth anniversary of the film's premiere, ticket sales, foreign rights, rentals, and sales of the movie worldwide totaled more than $840 million. And in the process, the fictional characters, story, and images of *Gone with the Wind* became firmly associated in the public's mind with the city of Atlanta.

SPORTS

Organized sports, yet another hallmark of a growing urban metropolis, became an increasingly popular diversion for Atlantans in the early twentieth century. At the top of the list, in terms of popularity and local fan support, was the "national pastime"—baseball. Organized baseball had made its first appearance in Atlanta back in 1866, when Captain Tom Burnett formed the Atlanta Baseball Club and faced off against a rival local team called the Gate City Nine. Burnett's team lost this initial contest 127–29 and he soon disbanded his club, but the Gate City Nine went on to finish their inaugural season with thirty-six wins and one loss (to the Dixie Club of Athens).

Professional baseball arrived in Atlanta nineteen years later in 1885, when the Southern League was formed with Henry Grady as its president. The league, which existed until 1900, featured teams from Atlanta, Augusta, Columbus, and Macon, Georgia; Birmingham, Alabama; and Chattanooga, Tennessee. Atlanta's baseball franchise won the Southern League championship in 1885, 1886, and 1895.

A new era of professional baseball began in Atlanta in 1901 with the formation of the Southern Association. This new league proved over the years to be one of the most stable in all of minor league baseball, with six of its charter teams remaining in the organization for fifty years or more. One of these long-lived teams was the Atlanta Crackers. Organized by New Orleans businessman Charles Abner Powell in 1902, the Crackers joined the new league that same year. (Also included in the league were the Birmingham Barons, the Chattanooga Lookouts, the Little Rock Travelers, the Memphis Chicks, the Mobile Bears, the Nashville Vols, and the New Orleans Pelicans.) Over the next four decades, the Crackers won nine league pennants and in 1938 became the first team in the league to achieve a "Grand Slam"—winning not only the league title but the All Star game, the Shaughnessy play-offs (featuring the league's four best teams), and the Dixie Series (which pitted the Southern Association Shaughnessy winners against the Shaughnessy champions of the Texas League). In the process, the Atlanta Crackers built a large and loyal following among both Atlanta's white and black baseball fans and gained financial support from sources like Coca-Cola Company president Robert Woodruff, who bought the team in 1933.

Good teams require good facilities, and, beginning in 1907, the Atlanta Crackers played their home games in what was considered one of the finest ballparks in the league—Ponce de Leon Park. Set on the site of an amusement park on Ponce de Leon Avenue, the ballpark featured a somewhat eccentric layout, with a fully grown magnolia tree and an embankment both situated in

An exhibition baseball game between the Atlanta Crackers and the Brooklyn Dodgers in Ponce de Leon Park, 1949. Jackie Robinson is on deck; this was the first time in the city's history that blacks and whites played together in a professional sport.

fair territory. In 1923, when the park's wooden stands burned down, R. J. Spiller, the ballpark's owner, replaced them with concrete stands with seating room for fourteen thousand and standing room for an additional six thousand fans. Spiller tried to christen the new structure with his own name, but fans and players over the years continued to refer to the field and the stadium as Ponce de Leon Park.

Baseball during this era in Atlanta, as elsewhere, remained racially segregated. No black baseball players were able to break the color line until Jackie Robinson joined the Brooklyn Dodgers in 1947. Two years later, Robinson appeared in an exhibition game at Ponce de Leon Park between the Crackers and the

Dodgers—the first time in Atlanta's history that blacks and whites competed together in an organized sport. (It would be another thirteen years before an integrated Atlanta baseball team and integrated seating were introduced to Ponce de Leon Park.)

In the absence of integrated teams and facilities, professional black athletes in early twentieth-century Atlanta joined all-black baseball teams like the Atlanta Deppens. These teams had toured the South before the turn of the century, playing other black baseball teams from New Orleans, Birmingham, Macon, and Chattanooga. The Deppens were later succeeded by the Atlanta Cubs, a semiprofessional team composed primarily of black college students from the Atlanta University schools. Many of the local fans referred to the Cubs as the "Black Crackers," and by 1920 the nickname had become so popular that the Cubs officially changed their name to the Atlanta Black Crackers. Some of the Black Crackers' home games were played at Ponce de Leon Park (when the white Crackers were out of town), but most of the time they played on fields located at local black schools like Morris Brown College and Morehouse College.

In the 1920s, the Black Crackers joined the newly formed Negro Southern League. Although teams in the league varied from year to year, they usually included the Atlanta Black Crackers, the Birmingham Black Barons, the Jacksonville Red Caps, the Memphis Red Sox, the Montgomery Grey Socks, the Nashville Elite Giants, and the New Orleans Crescent Stars. The Negro Southern League franchises were, for the most part, not as financially sound as those in the white Southern Association, and the lack of funds was evident in many areas. The visiting and home teams, for example, were each responsible for furnishing two balls per game, and games often had to be stopped to retrieve one of the balls. Gate receipts from the game went not only to the home team but also to the visiting team, as reimbursement for travel expenses. Moreover, since the teams could carry only twelve players, the athletes had to play more than one position, and membership on teams changed constantly.

In 1937, the financial problems of the Black Crackers eased somewhat when the team was bought by John and Bill Harden, owners of a gas station on Auburn Avenue. The Hardens not only provided their players with a more secure income (the average monthly salary for a player in the Negro Southern League was only $250), but acquired a bus and new uniforms for the team as well. The following year, the Black Crackers joined the Negro American League and won the league pennant and the Negro National Championship.

Despite the team's success, the Atlanta Black Crackers did not remain in the Negro American League beyond the 1938 season and instead affiliated once again with the Negro Southern League. The Southern League's days were numbered, however. Jackie Robinson's integration of the Dodgers the following decade opened baseball's major leagues to the region's best black players, and the Southern League was soon forced to disband. The Atlanta Black Crackers played their last season in 1949.

Football also proved to be an increasingly popular spectator sport in early twentieth-century Atlanta. Like baseball, football had made its first appearance in the city before the turn of the

Intercollegiate football was immediately popular in Atlanta when it was introduced in 1892. Here an exhibition game between Auburn University and the University of Georgia, played in Piedmont Park in 1895.

century. In fact, the state's first intercollegiate football game (between the University of Georgia and Auburn University) took place on February 20, 1892, at Piedmont Park. Auburn won the game 10–0, and despite the fact that none of the participants wore a helmet, there were no injuries. Five years later, however, a critical injury suffered in a University of Georgia football game nearly brought about the collapse of the intercollegiate sport in the state and region. In a game against the University of Virginia, Georgia fullback Richard Von Gammon sustained a blow to the head and died of a brain concussion. His death triggered a regional outcry against the sport. The tide of popular opinion soon turned, though, when the victim's mother wrote a letter to the University of Georgia Trustees stating her belief that her son would have wanted the sport to continue.

Georgia Institute of Technology's famous football rivalry with the University of Georgia also started in the late nineteenth century. The first game between these two Georgia schools occurred on the afternoon of November 4, 1893, in Athens and was won by Georgia Tech, 22–6. One of the stars of that game and the captain of the Tech team was Leonard Wood, a part-time student as well as the surgeon general at Fort McPherson. Five years after this inaugural game between Georgia and Georgia Tech, Wood saw action during the Spanish-American War as a commander in Teddy Roosevelt's "Rough Riders" and following the war served as governor-general of both Cuba and the Philippines. Eventually he became chief of staff of the army. In 1920, General Wood was also one of the leading Republican candidates for president before delegates turned instead to Warren G. Harding as a compromise candidate.

Atlanta's interest in football and in Tech football in particular increased during the next few decades as the "Ramblin' Wreck" became a regional and national football powerhouse. Under the leadership of Coach John Wilhelm Heisman, who had earlier coached at Auburn and Clemson Universities, Tech piled up an impressive record from 1904 to 1919 of 101 wins, 28 losses, and 6 ties. Included in this record were a stretch of 33 consecutive wins from 1915 to 1917 and a national championship in 1917.

Heisman not only produced a winning football program at Tech, he also helped revolutionize the game. It was Coach Heisman, for example, who introduced the shift (known as the "Heisman shift"); the center snap (previously the ball was rolled with the feet); the "hike" or "hut" vocal signal for starting play; jersey numbers; and scoreboards listing downs and yardage. He also lobbied for the adoption of the forward pass, which was finally legalized in 1906. (The Heisman trophy, which is given annually to the nation's best collegiate football player, is named in his honor.)

Football proved equally popular on Atlanta's black college campuses. Morehouse College organized its first football team in 1900, and within a few years was playing teams from Atlanta University, Fisk, Talladega, Tuskegee, and Hampton. During these early years of football, Morehouse went through a period of five seasons without a defeat and was generally regarded as one of the best black football teams in the region. Clark College established its first football team only one year after Morehouse (1901), but success on the gridiron generally eluded Clark until the 1920s. Then, under the guidance of Coach Samuel B. Taylor, Clark's "Black Battalion of Death" became a power to be reckoned with in the Southern Inter-Collegiate Athletic Conference. In 1928 Clark defeated the seemingly invincible "Golden Tigers" from Tuskegee, who had won forty-seven consecutive games to that point, and ended up as co-champions of their conference. Morris Brown came relatively late to organized football, forming its first team in 1911, but soon established an intense rivalry with Atlanta University (which dropped its athletic program in 1929 when it ceased offering an undergraduate curriculum) and with cross-campus opponent Clark College. A similar rivalry developed between Morehouse and Atlanta University. As a result, football games between these Atlanta University Center schools came to be eagerly anticipated annual events.

Golf also proved to be an increasingly popular sport in Atlanta during this period. The city's first golf course was established, with seven holes, at the Piedmont Driving Club in 1896. The professional assigned to oversee the course gave no lessons, but devoted most of his energies to supervising the caddies and the repair of members' golf clubs. Ten years later, another seven-hole course was constructed at the East Lake Country Club by the Atlanta Athletic Club, and in 1912, two more private golf and social clubs appeared in the exclusive residential communities of Ansley Park and Druid Hills. The city's private golf courses were not the only places where the game could be played, however. By the end of the 1920s, Atlanta was operating five public golf courses: Piedmont Park, Candler Park, James L. Key, Bobby Jones, and John A. White.

Atlanta was also home to a number of well-known golfing champions, including Perry Adair, who won the southern championship trophy in 1921, and Alexa Sterling, who captured the national women's amateur title in 1917, 1919, and 1920. The greatest golf hero in Atlanta during this period, however, was Robert Tyre Jones, Jr. Jones was born in Atlanta on March 17, 1902. In 1908, his family moved to a home near the thirteenth green of the East Lake golf course, where young Bobby Jones took up the game that would soon bring him worldwide fame. Three years later, at the age of nine, Jones won East Lake's Junior Championship. In 1916, Jones battled friend and fellow East Lake golfer Perry Adair in the newly organized Georgia State Amateur Championship and won the competition on the last green. That same year, Jones competed in his first United States Amateur Championship and reached the quarter finals before being eliminated—becoming the youngest player in the tournament's history to advance that far.

For the next five years, Bobby Jones won only two tournaments while he finished high school and received a degree from Georgia Tech. But in the period from 1923 to 1929, he dominated both British and American golf, winning the U.S. Open in 1923, 1926, and 1929; the United States Amateur in 1924, 1925, 1927, and 1928; and the British Open in 1926 and 1927. At the same time he was winning these tournaments, Jones also managed to complete a second bachelor of science degree at Harvard University, get married (to Mary Malone), enter law school at Emory University, gain admittance to the Georgia bar, and join an Atlanta law firm.

As successful as these remarkable years were, they were more than eclipsed by Jones's achievements in 1930, when he had what is arguably the best year in U.S. golf history. During that year, Jones won the Savannah Open and the Southeastern Open, and he captained the U.S. Walker golf team to victory in England. He also succeeded in winning the four most prestigious tournaments in golf at that time—the British Amateur, U.S. Open, British Open, and U.S. Amateur. Bobby Jones was the first golfer ever to win this "Grand Slam," and he quickly became a national and international sports hero. New York City honored him with a ticker-tape parade, and Atlanta followed with an even grander Bobby Jones Day parade down Peachtree Street. In fact, Atlanta proved so eager to honor its native son in 1930 that

Golfer Bobby Jones with trophies from his record-breaking Grand Slam in 1930. The feat has never been repeated nor could it be now, since some of the tournaments no longer have amateur standing.

humorist Will Rogers remarked, "Atlanta no more than gets cleaned up from one Bobby Jones celebration till another comes along. You can easily exist in Atlanta by eating only at Jones testimonial dinners."

Bobby Jones retired from tournament golf in 1930, the year of his greatest triumph. In his fourteen-year career, he had played in only fifty-two tournaments (fewer than most professional golfers of today play in two years on the circuit) but had won twenty-three. Even in retirement, Bobby Jones remained an influential force in the game. He was president of the Atlanta Athletic Club and the Peachtree Golf Club, and he codesigned the Augusta National Golf Course, host site of the popular annual Masters tournament. He also produced short films on golfing fundamentals featuring well-known Hollywood actors and wrote several books on the subject.

In 1948, after being diagnosed with syringomyelia, a degenerative spinal ailment, Bobby Jones was forced to quit playing the game he loved. He continued, however, in his other career pursuits as a lawyer and as an executive in several local business ventures. He died in Atlanta on December 18, 1971.

Public Parks and Amusement Parks

Atlantans' growing infatuation with sports in the early decades of the twentieth century was reflected in the increasing number of recreational facilities to be found in the city. At the turn of the century, two large public parks had already been established in Atlanta—Grant Park (donated to the city by Colonel Lemuel Pratt Grant in 1882) and Piedmont Park (site of the 1887 Piedmont Exposition and the 1895 Cotton States and International Exposition, and purchased by the city in 1904)—as well as a number of smaller neighborhood parks, such as Springvale (in Inman Park) and Mims Park (in northwest Atlanta). During the first two decades of the twentieth century, additional park space in the residential communities of West End, Ansley Park, Druid Hills, and Candler Park were purchased by the city and put under the supervision of Atlanta's park commission.

These new public parks added much needed green space to the expanding city and also provided new recreational facilities, such as baseball fields, tennis courts, and swimming pools. Linked by streetcar lines to the rest of the city, Atlanta's public parks and golf courses became the locus for a widening range of outdoor sports activities.

The parks, however, were not open to all Atlantans. In fact, African Americans found their access to these parks increasingly restricted by Jim Crow laws, regulations, and customs at the same time that the number of public parks and recreational options were on the rise. As a result, black Atlantans and organizations like the Neighborhood Union (founded by Lugenia Burns Hope) pushed the city to create public parks and spaces that could be utilized by the city's African American communities. In

The Neighborhood Union in 1925, founded by Lugenia Burns Hope (seated, center) to bring about social reform and neighborhood improvements in the city's black communities.

1922, the city finally authorized the construction of Washington Park, the first public park for Atlanta's black citizens. Located on the west side of the city in an area developed by black businessman, realtor, and builder Heman Perry, Washington Park contained many of the same recreational facilities found in Atlanta's parks for whites, including the city's first public swimming pool for African Americans.

Another type of public park—the amusement park—also proved to be a popular recreational pursuit for Atlantans in the early twentieth century. One of the most frequently attended of these sites was Ponce de Leon Park, built on the grounds of a nineteenth-century resort and picnic area called Ponce de Leon Springs. In 1906, the Ponce de Leon Park Association spent some $50,000 converting the resort into a new amusement center complete with a midway, a skating rink, picnic grounds, and rides. (One year later, the park would also become home to the Atlanta Crackers baseball team.)

Another popular amusement area, Lakewood Park, was located on the southwest side of the city. Lakewood, which contained some 375 acres of largely undeveloped woodland, had hosted an amusement park since 1894. In 1916, it became the site of a far larger enterprise—the Southeastern Fair. New buildings were constructed within the park to house the fair's many proposed exhibits, shows, and performances, and in its inaugural year, the Southeastern Fair offered visitors art, livestock, agricultural, and farm machinery exhibits; an automobile show; a women's suffrage demonstration; and a fireworks display. Although it would later encounter some tough times during the Depression, the fair survived and continued to be a popular attraction for decades to follow before it finally closed in 1978.

MUNICIPAL SERVICES

As Atlanta's population increased and its borders expanded during the early twentieth century, the city's municipal services strained to keep up with the growth. In 1910, more than eighty miles of Atlanta's streets still lacked water mains or sewer lines; two-thirds of the streets were unpaved; sewage disposal in general was inadequate and haphazard; water pressure in the city's lines was frequently too low to fight fires; the city's main public hospital, Grady, could not keep up with the increasing demands on its services; and only about one-half of Atlanta's student-age population was enrolled in the city's overcrowded and dilapidated public schools. To help remedy this situation, Atlanta residents passed a $3 million bond issue in 1910, the largest in the city's history to that date. The strain on the city's systems continued, however, and in 1919 Atlanta attempted to pass an additional bond referendum to upgrade, improve, and extend its municipal services. It was finally passed two years later.

Perhaps nowhere was the strain on the city's systems more obvious (and dangerous) than in the area of fire protection. The city's first professional fire department had been organized back in 1882, but the widespread use of flammable building materials, the lack of enforceable fire codes, and problems with the city's water lines handicapped fire-fighting efforts for decades to come. In 1917, all of these factors came into play when Atlanta experienced a conflagration that proved far more destructive than Sherman's famous leveling of the city during the Civil War.

The Great Fire of 1917 appears to have started around noon on May 21, in an area north of Decatur Street between Fort and Hilliard Streets. After wreaking havoc in the surrounding black residential section near Auburn Avenue, the fire swept northeast across Boulevard Avenue and destroyed homes and structures in the white middle-class neighborhood located there. Firefighters from as far away as Birmingham, Columbus, and Chattanooga traveled to Atlanta to help with the battle, but the fire continued to spread until authorities dynamited houses along Ponce de Leon Avenue to establish an effective fire break. After ten hours of burning, the fire was finally brought under control, but damage to public and private property had been extensive. Over three hundred acres (fifty blocks) of the city had been leveled by the fire. Approximately two thousand buildings were destroyed and ten thousand people

The 1917 fire shown in the act of destroying some of the fifty city blocks it claimed, including these homes in the Old Fourth Ward near Auburn Avenue.

made homeless. The total damage from the fire to city and private property was estimated at $5.5 million.

The city's social welfare programs also proved insufficient to meet the population's growing needs. Atlanta did cover some of the expenses for the indigent at Grady Hospital and cooperated with the state in the operation of the Battle Hill Tuberculosis Hospital and the Confederate Veterans Home. But there were relatively few official city agencies dedicated to assisting the poor and even fewer whose caseload included African Americans. In fact, it was 1908 before the city established its first social service agencies and programs for black Atlantans. In the absence of city assistance, black community needs were met (as they had been during the nineteenth century) primarily through the actions of individuals or the programs of a growing array of black self-help, fraternal, and religious organizations. Prominent among these were individuals such as Carrie Steele Logan, who founded the city's first black orphanage in 1889; self-help agencies like the Neighborhood Union, which established health centers, boys' and girls' clubs, and vocational classes for children and lobbied for improved public facilities for African Americans; and fraternal organizations like the Odd Fellows and the Good Samaritans, who raised thousands of dollars for the poor and infirm of the city.

The black churches of Atlanta also organized programs to meet the pressing social and economic needs of their communities. The First Congregational Church of Atlanta, under the leadership of Reverend Henry Hugh Proctor, for example, sponsored a home for black working women, business and cooking schools, a kindergarten, and an employment bureau. Similar community services and programs were provided by the city's other prominent black churches, such as Big Bethel A.M.E. Church and Ebenezer and Wheat Street Baptist Churches.

While impoverished white Atlantans may have had more access to city programs and agencies than their black counterparts, Atlanta was not especially generous to either group. In fact, the most active agent for social service was not a city agency at all, but the Community Chest, which combined the programs of thirty-nine different local charities. But even the Community Chest's efforts proved insufficient as the Depression loomed and demands on the organization increased. In 1929, more than 197,000 private individuals and families were assisted by the Chest. The organization's attempts to raise $480,000 for relief failed, however, and in 1930 Atlanta ranked last among similarly sized cities in terms of its per capita expenditures for welfare programs.

EDUCATION

PUBLIC SCHOOLS — Public education was another area in which the needs and demands of Atlanta's growing population quickly outstripped the existing facilities. As mentioned earlier, in 1910 only about one-half of the city's student-age population attended school. The absence of a compulsory attendance law, coupled with weak and poorly enforced child-labor regulations, meant that many impoverished children did not go to school and instead assisted their families by working in area mills and factories. The fact that Atlanta did not provide free textbooks to its pupils until the 1920s also discouraged school attendance among the poor. Even those students who did attend the city's public schools were frequently housed in overcrowded, dilapidated, unsanitary structures with budgets as meager as their facilities.

The widespread overcrowding that occurred in Atlanta's public school system during the first decade of the twentieth century meant that most schools utilized double sessions (each lasting part of a day) to accommodate the demand. In 1914, after intense pressure from white, middle-class parents, the city finally eliminated the double sessions and restricted class size to forty-five students in the white public schools. Nevertheless, problems associated with overcrowding, insufficient funding and supplies, and outdated facilities continued to surface during the 1920s and 1930s.

Each of these problems was even more acute in the city's black public schools. Since its establishment in 1872, the Atlanta Board of Education had placed a low value on the education of blacks. In fact, in 1913 the board proposed eliminating the seventh and eighth grades altogether in the city's black schools, arguing that such a level of education was unnecessary for students most likely to find future employment as manual laborers. Although this proposal was defeated, there were no public high schools for African Americans anywhere in the city until Booker T. Washington High School (which initially also included seventh and eighth grades) was opened on the west side in 1924. Not surprisingly, given the board's orientation, expenditures for the city's black schools remained much lower than the monies allocated for white schools. As late as 1940, for example, the average amount expended on Atlanta's African American students was one-third of the average amount allocated for white students. Black teachers also continued to be paid less than their white counterparts (and women less than men), and the city's

The city's first public high school for African Americans was named after Booker T. Washington, who is also commemorated in a statue by renowned sculptor Charles Keck in front of the building.

black public schools were more likely than white schools to be without kindergartens, auditoriums, gymnasiums, and cafeterias.

That the African American community in Atlanta was able to secure a public high school for its children at all was primarily due to the organizational skills and growing political strength of the city's black leadership. Since 1892, local Democratic officials had made use of a "white primary" law to effectively restrict voting in primary elections to white males. This ordinance, which was utilized throughout the South to limit the voting power of African Americans, minimized black influence within the Democratic Party—by far the most dominant and powerful political party in the region. But while African Americans in Atlanta were excluded from primary elections, they could still vote in special elections, such as school bond referendums. In 1902 and again in 1909, the black community supported proposed bond issues in the hope that some of the money would be applied to their schools. The bond issues passed, but the school board refused to allocate additional funds for black schools as requested. In 1917, local NAACP leaders again came before the board, asking for improved facilities, but again they were rebuffed. Finally, in 1919, distrustful of city hall and school board promises, black Atlantans used their vote to help defeat two proposed school bond measures. Two years later, when a $4 million school bond referendum again came up for a vote, black leaders promised support for the measure only if their demands for a new public high school were met. The referendum passed, and Booker T. Washington High School was finally built.

Just how desperately a black public high school was needed and how much it was appreciated by the Atlanta African American community was quickly evident once Washington High School opened its doors. As the only black secondary school in the metropolitan area, Washington High drew students not just from Atlanta but also from the surrounding communities of East Point, College Park, Decatur, and Marietta. Moreover, since there had been no earlier opportunity for black students to progress past elementary school (except through tuition-based classes at Atlanta University), some of the first students at Washington were well beyond the normal age range for its classes. Thus several eighteen- and nineteen-year-olds enrolled in the school's seventh- and eighth-grade classes, and students were the same age as the teachers in some of the upper-level grades.

Race was not the only factor that served to segregate Atlanta's public schools in the early twentieth century. Many of the city's public high schools were also divided by gender and by curriculum. Boys' High School and Girls' High School, which were founded in 1872, were the flagships of the Atlanta school system and featured a rigorous curriculum of classics, mathematics, and languages. Tech High, founded in 1909 for boys, was a bit more vocationally oriented in its subjects, although it featured college prep courses as well. Commercial High School, established six years later, was similar to Tech in its curriculum. It was also the city's first coeducational high school. When Booker T. Washington High was finally opened in 1924, it incorporated all of the features of Atlanta's four white high schools, providing both academic and vocational training in a coeducational setting. Students at Washington High not only took courses in biology, chemistry, physics, math (algebra, trigonometry, and calculus), English composition, history, and economics, but also were offered training in such areas as tailoring, brick masonry, home nursing, cooking, and cafeteria management.

The appointment of Dr. Willis A. Sutton (former principal of Tech High) to the position of city school superintendent in 1921 and changes in the city's approach to public education brought about additional reforms in Atlanta's public schools. Sutton, who later became president of the National Education Association, encouraged and supported the introduction of new subjects into the schools' curricula, such as music (including bands, orchestras, and vocal choirs), arts, crafts, and drama. He also helped restrict somewhat the widespread and frequent use of corporal punishment by teachers and administrators. The passage of a compulsory school attendance law in 1920, coupled with the distribution of free textbooks and strengthened child-labor laws later in the decade, dramatically improved another problem area for Atlanta's schools. By 1940, approximately 90 percent of the city's school-age children were enrolled in school.

These progressive changes, however, could do little to ameliorate the biggest challenges to Atlanta's public school system in the 1920s and 1930s—continued overcrowding and shrinking financial resources. At Washington High, for example, temporary wooden structures were built in the 1930s to house an overflow student population and double sessions were reintroduced. The tremendous increase in students at Washington and other schools in Atlanta put additional strain on an already financially distressed system. Despite city charter amendments in 1918 and 1922 that guaranteed a fixed percentage of municipal revenues for the public school system, the Atlanta Board of Education continued to run out of funds. As the situation worsened during the Depression, teachers were forced to take a series of drastic pay cuts. Finally things reached the point where the city could not pay the teachers at all and instead issued them scrip—promissory notes that the city would pay them when it was able. Fortunately for the teachers, Rich's department store agreed to accept the scrip for cash, an action that earned the store the undying loyalty of many city employees.

PRIVATE SCHOOLS — At the same time that Atlanta's public school system was experiencing growing pains, a number of private educational institutions were also emerging within the metropolitan area. In 1900, for example, the Georgia Military Academy opened in College Park with a student enrollment of forty and a faculty comprised of Colonel John C. Woodward and one assistant. Later the school was renamed Woodward Academy and a junior college department was added to its offerings. Another military day school, Marist College, was founded in 1901 in downtown Atlanta by the Marist Order of the Roman Catholic Church. Eight years later, the North Avenue Presbyterian School, which several decades later would establish a college preparatory school for boys named Westminster, was opened.

A number of other private colleges and universities also found a home in the budding metropolis. In 1916, for example, Oglethorpe University, which had once been located in downtown Atlanta and had closed its doors in 1872 due to financial difficulties, reemerged at a new location along Peachtree Road in the city's suburbs (its present-day site). Dr. Thornwell Jacobs, a minister and grandson of an Oglethorpe mathematics professor, succeeded in raising almost half a million dollars to fund the school's construction. He also managed to enlist the generous support of William Randolph Hearst, nationally known newspaper magnate and owner of the *Atlanta Georgian* newspaper. Over a thirty-year period, Hearst contributed more than $400,000 to the school and helped Oglethorpe gain control of four hundred acres of land surrounding the university, including Silver Lake, which was renamed Lake Phoebe in honor of Hearst's mother.

Another school that moved its campus to the Atlanta area was

Emory University. And, as in the case of Oglethorpe, a million-aire played an important role in the school's move. This time the benefactor was Asa G. Candler, owner and guiding force of the Coca-Cola Company.

In 1913, the General Conference of the Methodist Episcopal Church, South, decided it needed a new university in the region and established an educational commission to pursue the matter. Two brothers on the commission—Warren A. Candler and Asa Candler—took the lead in seeing that the new university was located in Atlanta and that a transplanted Emory College (origi-nally located in Oxford, Georgia) formed the basis of the uni-versity's "academic department." (Warren Candler, a Methodist bishop and chair of the commission, had earlier served as presi-dent of Emory College, and his older brother, Asa, had been selected as a trustee for the school.)

To help seal the school's move to Atlanta and its selection as the conference's new university, Asa Candler pledged $1 million to endow the school and seventy-five acres of land in the emerg-ing subdivision of Druid Hills as a site of the university's campus. Persuaded by these generous offers, Emory moved to its new home in 1919, where schools of theology, medicine, and law were soon in operation. (The liberal arts division of the school remained for the time being in Oxford, although it would later relocate to Atlanta as well. Emory-at-Oxford remains a two-year liberal arts college.) Bishop Warren Candler served as the first chancellor of the new university.

Eight years later, in 1927, another theological school relo-cated to the Atlanta area when the Columbia Theological Seminary established its present-day campus in Decatur. Columbia had begun its existence in Lexington, Georgia, as the Theological Seminary of the (Presbyterian) Synod of South Carolina and Georgia, but had moved to Columbia, South Carolina, shortly after its founding. In the 1920s a campaign was undertaken to relocate the school to a more central loca-tion in the region, and the $500,000 raised in the Atlanta area for equipment and endowment helped direct the seminary to the city's environs.

TENSIONS AMIDST THE GROWTH

THE 1906 RACE RIOT — As the first decades of the twentieth century unfolded, Atlanta grew quickly in size and regional stature. The city, already firmly established as a regional rail center, was fast becoming a commercial capital as well, and the promise of new jobs and opportunities brought thousands of newcomers to Atlanta. There were undercurrents of tension in this period of rapid growth, however, and they manifested themselves in periodic outbursts of violence and hostility.

One of the earliest and most violent of these episodes was the 1906 race riot. Racial tensions during that year had been intensified by a long and bitter campaign for governor in which the winner, Hoke Smith, the one-time president and publisher of the *Atlanta Journal*, called for the disfranchisement of black citizens through a constitutional amendment. His opponent, Clark Howell, a former editor of the *Atlanta Constitution*, also publicly opposed black political "equality," but felt that the white primary system was a sufficient guard against such a "threat." One month after Smith's election, the city erupted in the worst race riot ever to occur in Atlanta. On the heels of incendiary news reports alleging black assaults on white women, angry white mobs attacked black citizens in their homes and businesses, on the streets and in the streetcars. The rioting began the evening of September 22 and lasted until the next night. Atlanta was put under martial law, and calm was not restored to the city until September 26.

It is difficult to determine how many Atlantans lost their lives in this riot, as the estimates of the numbers killed and wounded vary widely among contemporary accounts. The official total (which is probably far too low) was twelve dead—ten black and two white; and seventy injured—sixty black and ten white. There is less uncertainty, however, about the impact of this disturbance on black housing and business patterns in the city. The riot clearly hastened the city's move toward the economic exclusion and residential segregation of African Americans. Following the riot, African Americans were more likely to settle in established black

The state militia was called out to restore order during the Atlanta race riot of 1906. Scores of blacks were killed; many more blacks and whites were injured. The race riot represented the nadir of Atlanta race relations.

communities, particularly those located on the eastern fringe of downtown in the Old Fourth Ward or on the west side of the city near Atlanta University. And black businesses, some of which had once been interspersed among white commercial concerns on Peachtree Street, were now increasingly located to the east on Auburn Avenue.

Modest efforts to promote biracial understanding followed in the wake of the riot, culminating in the formation of the Commission on Interracial Cooperation (CIC) in 1919. An offshoot of the CIC was the Association of Southern Women for the Prevention of Lynching (ASWPL), organized by Jessie Daniel Ames (chair of the Texas Interracial Commission) in 1930 and based in Atlanta. Neither of these interracial organizations, however, struck at the underlying premise of Jim Crow—that blacks and whites should remain separate. (The ASWPL, for all its noble aims, did not even include black women among its members.)

As the century progressed, efforts to segregate African Americans in Atlanta continued and expanded. In 1913, for example, Atlanta became the first city in Georgia to try to extend segregation to housing patterns through use of a residential segregation ordinance. Although this law was struck down by the state supreme court two years later, the Atlanta City Council passed a similar statute in 1917 (that was also ruled unconstitutional) and in 1922 hired an urban planner from Cleveland, Ohio, to draw up a comprehensive zoning ordinance for the city that included residential zones based upon race. This zoning plan received the support of the state legislature and was strengthened by a 1928 amendment to the Georgia constitution that allowed residential zoning. Though Atlanta's racial zoning plan was finally struck down by the Georgia Supreme Court, this defeat did not spell the end of segregated residential districts in the city. Instead, for the next few decades, the city would maintain Jim Crow segregation through extralegal pressures and the equally effective tool of restrictive covenants—agreements between private parties or property owners that established limitations on the sale of property to particular groups—most notably African Americans and Jews.

THE LEO FRANK TRIAL AND ATLANTA'S JEWISH COMMUNITY — The 1906 race riot had exposed some of the racial tensions present in early twentieth-century Atlanta. Less than a decade later, another violent episode in the city's history—the trial and lynching of Leo Frank—brought to the surface growing class and religious antagonisms that were in turn linked to dramatic changes taking place in the city's population and labor force.

Industrialization and urbanization combined early in the century to swell Atlanta's population and remake its workforce. Drawn by the lure of available employment in the city's factories and businesses, thousands of men and women flocked to Atlanta during the first two decades of the century, doubling the city's population in the process. As the pool of available applicants for jobs broadened, the makeup of the workforce also changed. One of the most obvious changes was the increased presence of women in the workplace. By 1920, 42 percent of all Atlanta women aged sixteen and older had joined the workforce (a rate of female employment exceeded only in Washington, D.C., and in the Massachusetts textile cities of Fall River, Lowell, and New Bedford). Even more significant was the number of white women entering the job market during this period. In 1900, this group made up only 28 percent of the total number of female wage earners in Atlanta; by 1920, they comprised 48 percent of the total and were present in great numbers in fields such as clerical and textile work. Atlanta's black female wage earners, on the other hand, found fewer and fewer opportunities for work in the city's factories and businesses, and instead found themselves increasingly confined to laundry and domestic work.

The opportunities for employment and business growth in turn-of-the-century Atlanta also drew newcomers from abroad, including an increasing number of Jewish immigrants from Eastern Europe. Jews had been present in Atlanta since its beginnings and had played an important role in the city's business, civic, and political life. Jewish residents, for example, were responsible for establishing such important local businesses as Rich's department store and the Fulton Bag and Cotton Mill and had played a leading role in developing the city's public school system, establishing Grady Hospital and the Piedmont Sanitorium (later Piedmont Hospital), and bringing the grand opera to Atlanta. Despite their small numbers (less than 3 percent of the total population in 1910), Atlanta Jews had also played a prominent role in the city's politics. Aaron Haas, for example, had served as councilman and alderman of the city and as the first mayor pro tem in 1875 and was one of about a dozen Jewish leaders who held political office in Atlanta in the period between 1874 and 1911.

At the turn of the century, however, the composition of the Jewish community in Atlanta began to change. Traditionally, most of the Jewish residents in Atlanta had emigrated from Western Europe—particularly Germany. In 1880, for example, 600 of the 612 Jews in the city were German. During the next decade, however, an increasing number of Jewish immigrants arrived from Russia and other Eastern European locales. By 1896, there were already 317 Russian Jews in the city, most of them living around Decatur Street, where they established businesses or found employment. Beginning in 1911, a third group of Jews immigrated to Atlanta, Sephardic Jews from Turkey and the Greek Isle of Rhodes. This influx of new settlers from Eastern Europe and the old Ottoman Empire not only increased the number of Jews in Atlanta but also dramatically altered the makeup of the Jewish community. By 1910 the German Jewish population in the city stood at 1,400; the number of Jewish residents from Eastern Europe, however, was 2,400 (one-third of Atlanta's entire foreign-born population).

The differences between Atlanta's traditional Jewish community and the new immigrants were reflected in a myriad of ways. Most of the German Jews, for example, were members of the Reform branch of Judaism and emphasized the importance of assimilation into the larger Atlanta community, even conducting their synagogue services in English. The newly arrived Eastern European Jews, on the other hand, tended to be Orthodox in their religious beliefs, with customs and languages that were alien to many Atlantans. Finally, the Sephardic Jews brought with them customs, speech, and religious practices that differed from both the German and the Eastern European communities. These religious differences within the Jewish community were further underscored by social barriers erected between the groups. The prestigious Standard Club, for example, established by the German Jews in 1904, refused membership to either the city's Eastern European or Sephardic Jews. The older German community also tended to resent the refusal or inability of the new Jewish immigrant groups to assimilate and feared that their "distinctiveness" might jeopardize the position and influence of the more established Jewish leaders.

Despite the dramatic divisions and differences within the city's Jewish community, many non-Jewish Atlantans tended to view the Jewish population as a monolithic whole and blamed the Jews for the various "evils" of industrialization (including the employment of vulnerable white southern women), since they owned or managed some of the city's largest mills and fac-

The two protagonists of one of Atlanta's most tragic events: Mary Phagan was murdered in 1913, and her boss, Leo Frank, was tried, convicted, and later lynched for her murder. Frank was pardoned in 1986.

tories. As nativist and anti-Semitic opinions gained prominence in the early twentieth century, they found expression in a number of venues—editorials, cartoons, vaudeville acts, and even movies playing in Atlanta. They reached their fever pitch, however, during the trial of Leo Frank.

In July 1913, Leo Frank, a prominent member of the German Jewish community and a National Pencil Company superintendent, was arrested and charged with assaulting and murdering a thirteen-year-old white female employee named Mary Phagan. In a highly charged atmosphere marked by sensationalist press coverage and virulent anti-Semitism, Frank was found guilty of the crime and sentenced to death. (Ironically, the prosecution's chief witness against Leo Frank was James Conley, a black custodian in the factory, and Frank's trial was one of the few times in that era that the testimony of a black man was used to convict a white man.) As national Jewish organizations rushed to Frank's defense, the case quickly became a national and international *cause célèbre*. Frank's lawyers continued to appeal the conviction, citing the mob atmosphere during the trial, but in April 1915 the U.S. Supreme Court denied a plea to reverse the decision, and Frank's sentence was upheld. His lawyers had also appealed to Governor John M. Slaton, however, to commute

Frank's sentence, and on June 21, 1915 (two days before his term ended), Governor Slaton commuted Frank's sentence to life imprisonment.

Local reaction to the commutation was quick and in many instances hostile. Tom Watson, editor of *The Jeffersonian* and a future U.S. senator from Georgia, declared in his newspaper that the governor had sold out to the Jews and urged Atlantans to lynch Frank and "get the governor." Some apparently took Watson's advice to heart, and two companies of the National Guard as well as county police had to be called out to protect the governor's Buckhead mansion. (Twenty-six men carrying pistols and dynamite were arrested.) Slaton escaped injury (by leaving the country for an extended European vacation), but Leo Frank was less fortunate. On the evening of August 16, twenty-five armed men who called themselves the "Knights of Mary Phagan" broke into his jail cell at Milledgeville and carted him off to Marietta, where they lynched him.

THE KU KLUX KLAN — The impact of the Leo Frank trial and lynching was felt on the local, regional, and national level. The publicity surrounding the case, for example, helped establish the fame and reputations of some individuals who were only peripherally associated with the trial, including Tom Watson and country musician Fiddlin' John Carson, whose song "The Ballad of Mary Phagan" became a regional classic. The case also brought about changes at the factory where Mary Phagan and Leo Frank were employed. Following the trial, Sigmund Montag, owner of the National Pencil Company, shifted to a predominately black male operating workforce (which in turn gave way to an increasingly black female workforce during World War I). Finally, the case directly contributed to the establishment of two disparate but important national organizations—the Anti-Defamation League of B'nai B'rith and a revived and reinvigorated Ku Klux Klan.

On Thanksgiving Day 1915 (some four months after Leo Frank's death), thirty-four men gathered atop Stone Mountain to bring back to life the Reconstruction-era vigilante organization known as the Ku Klux Klan. A few weeks later, the group made use of the Atlanta showing of D. W. Griffith's classic film, *Birth of a Nation*, to both publicize their cause and increase their local membership. Draped in sheets and mounted on horseback, the founding members of the recreated KKK paraded down Peachtree Street on December 6, 1915, firing guns into the air and exhorting their white brethren to help save, reform, and protect the South. How much Griffith's film, which glorified the exploits of the earlier Ku Klux Klan and vilified black southerners' attempts to gain political and social equality, contributed to the contemporary organization's growth is difficult to say. But it is clear that the film struck a resonant chord among white audiences in Atlanta. The Atlanta Theater, where the film was shown, held the movie over for an unprecedented second and third week, and local journalists estimated that 19,000 Atlantans saw the film during the first week alone (with 300–1,000 people being turned away at each matinee showing) and that 35,000—about one-fourth of the city's white population—had seen the film by the end of the second week.

Even more dramatic than the large numbers of white Atlantans who saw the film was the reaction of these viewers to Griffith's story. Atlanta film critics described scenes in which audience members (and the critics themselves) cheered, clapped, and jumped to their feet in either approval or indignation. One showing of the film, attended by more than a hundred Confederate veterans, even elicited an authentic rebel yell from the audience members.

Led by William J. Simmons, a former preacher and organizer for a national fraternal order called the Woodmen of the World, the revived Ku Klux Klan quickly grew and spread its nativist message of opposition to Jews, Catholics, and racial equality. The KKK also operated in many localities as a vigilante enforcer of local morality, selectively punishing drunkards, adulterers, and wife beaters in addition to terrorizing African Americans. By 1924, the Klan had expanded far beyond its southern base with "Klaverns," or branches, in almost every northern state and a reported national membership of six million.

Locally, the Klan was a very prominent force during the 1920s and 1930s. Atlanta served as the headquarters or "Imperial City" of the Invisible Empire for almost a decade after the Klan's inception, and in 1921 the Klan purchased an elegant home at the corner of Peachtree Road and East Wesley Road that served as its "Imperial Palace." By 1923, membership in the city's Nathan Bedford Forrest Klan No. 1 stood at over fifteen thousand and included notable Atlanta businessmen, educators, clergy, judges, policemen, and politicians. Although the Klan's influence waned somewhat in the late 1920s, the tensions and economic uncertainties of the Depression kept the organization alive, and it remained a powerful extralegal force in the city, dedicated to maintaining and enforcing Jim Crow restrictions and practices.

THE NEW WOMAN

Despite the efforts of organizations like the Ku Klux Klan to promote and maintain a nineteenth-century southern racial and social order, the traditional role and status of southern women were clearly changing in the early twentieth century. The entrance of more Atlanta women into the workforce and women's involvement in temperance, education, and prison reform movements led to calls for political equality for women and for the vote. These demands for equal suffrage, it should be noted, had both a class and racial cast to them. The women's organizations and suffrage societies that lobbied most for the vote were primarily composed of white, urban women of the middle and upper classes. In the city's separate black women's organizations, on the other hand, there was little support of or interest in the suffrage question. To be sure, some individual leaders (like Lugenia Burns Hope) were suffrage sympathizers, but many other African American women appear to have viewed the equal suffrage campaign as a white woman's issue. And even those local black women who did support the movement realized that their power as voters was likely to be limited by the same Jim Crow laws and restrictions that had served to disfranchise black males.

The equal suffrage movement in Atlanta had its beginnings in the late nineteenth century. In 1894, a women's suffrage league was formed, and the following year the National American

Woman Suffrage Association, led by Susan B. Anthony, held its annual meeting in the city. In 1902, a formal request was made to the Atlanta City Council to grant women the right to vote, but the request was denied. The issue did not die, however, and instead gained both national and local momentum. In 1913, two more women's suffrage organizations appeared in the city—the Georgia Equal Suffrage League and the Georgia Men's League for Woman Suffrage. Success for the suffragists finally came in May 1919 when the Democratic Executive Committee of Atlanta voted 24–1 to give women the vote in municipal elections. The following month, an amendment to the U.S. Constitution granting women the franchise was sent to the states for approval. The Georgia legislature voted against the proposal (and did not officially ratify the amendment until 1970), but the Nineteenth Amendment to the U.S. Constitution became law anyway, taking effect on August 20, 1920.

STRIKES — Urbanization, industrialization, and the growth of a permanent working class did more than just intensify class and religious antagonisms within the city, as reflected in the Leo Frank case. These forces also raised important questions regarding the rights of workers, the responsibilities of employers, and the role of unions in labor/management negotiations. These and related issues increasingly became matters of public debate as a series of labor strikes broke out in Atlanta's textile, streetcar, and automobile manufacturing industries during the first four decades of the twentieth century.

In Atlanta, as elsewhere in the industrialized South, textile mills became the locus of much labor unrest. Walkouts and work stoppages occurred in mills throughout the region as labor attempted to secure better pay and better working conditions. Despite the assistance of national labor unions and the sympathetic writings of journalists, who focused their attention on the large numbers of women and children employed in the industry, these strikes were largely unsuccessful. Atlanta had few laws to guide or control negotiations, and employers (particularly in urban areas) could frequently draw from a ready pool of unemployed labor to replace striking workers. The 1914 strike at Atlanta's Fulton Bag and Cotton Mill, the city's largest textile mill, was in many ways characteristic of this trend.

Fulton Bag and Cotton was founded in 1889 by Jacob Elsas, who built houses for his employees in an area first known as "The Factory Lot" and later as "Cabbagetown." By 1914, the mill had branch offices throughout the country and employed some 1,300 people in its Atlanta factory—35 percent of whom were women and 12 percent of whom were boys and girls under sixteen years of age. The first stirrings of labor unrest at the mill occurred in October 1913 when several hundred weavers and loom fixers staged a work stoppage to protest the firing of a loom fixer and management's decision to require an even longer period of notice when workers quit. (According to the contracts employees were required to sign, the company was not responsible for work-related injuries and could discharge workers at any time. Employees, on the other hand, were financially responsible for damage to machinery, could be fined for minor infractions, and were required to give notice before they quit or forfeit a week's wages.) In May 1914, workers at Fulton Bag and Cotton Mill again walked off their jobs, this time to protest Elsas's firing of union employees. Initially, the strikers demanded only the reinstatement of the discharged workers, but as the strike continued, their grievances expanded to include calls for higher wages, shorter hours, an end to child labor, and termination of the dreaded labor contracts.

The United Textile Workers Union of America (UTW), which had formed Local No. 886 at the mill in the wake of the 1913 work stoppage, sent organizers to the city (as did the American Federation of Labor) and set up tents to house those evicted from their jobs and their factory-owned homes. Journalists and local organizations like the Men and Religion Forward Movement focused public attention on the plight of women and child laborers and demanded of mill employers a "living wage" that would enable a man to support his wife and children and keep them out of the factories. Despite this attention and support, the strike eventually collapsed, and in May 1915, the UTW closed its camps and admitted defeat.

In 1934, another, much larger textile strike met with a similar end when workers in the mills of Atlanta and throughout the region took part in a nationwide strike to protest violations of the National Industrial Recovery Act. Thus, while New Deal legislation brought about the national recognition of unions and gave workers the right to organize, poor working conditions, low wages, and a decidedly hostile anti-union climate continued to predominate in most mills in Atlanta and elsewhere throughout the South.

There were areas of union strength in Atlanta, however, particularly in the transportation industries, where workers were a bit more successful during the early twentieth century in gaining recognition of their unions and better working conditions. In 1916, for example, hundreds of Atlanta streetcar workers walked off their jobs, launching one of the most tumultuous strikes in the city's history. In the ensuing labor dispute, which was marked by violence (including a wave of dynamiting), the workers did not achieve their immediate demands, but they did gain widening public support and even influenced local elections to some extent. Two years later, another strike of streetcar operatives occurred, and this time the workers were more successful. After National War Labor Board hearings on the strike in 1919, the local streetcar company signed a contract with Local No. 732, reinstated some of the union men who had been fired, and agreed to improve working conditions. The importance and influence of unions in the streetcar industry was further underscored two years later when the Amalgamated Association of Street and Electric Employees of America held its international convention in Atlanta.

As significant as these two streetcar strikes were, it was a work stoppage in a local General Motors plant in 1936 that had the greatest national impact. On November 18, 1936, workers at the Lakewood General Motors and Fisher body plants shut down the assembly lines in protest over pay scales, working hours, the absence of overtime pay, and management's refusal to negotiate with the United Automobile Workers union (Local No. 34). Following the assembly line shutdown, workers in the plant stayed in the building, occupying the factory overnight and into the next morning. The workers finally exited after receiving assurances from management that the factory would not resume operations until the labor issues could be resolved. This historic occasion marked the first sit-down strike in the automobile industry and launched a series of General Motors plant closings and strikes across the nation, culminating in the famous Flint, Michigan, sit-down strike of 1937. The local strike at the Lakewood plant lasted a little more than three months and ended when management finally agreed to recognize the local union. Changes in pay and working conditions followed shortly thereafter.

TRANSPORTATION

THE RAILROADS — The same transportation industries that experienced strikes and labor unrest in the early twentieth century

The new terminal station, erected in 1905 and demolished in 1971. The station moved passenger train traffic to the outskirts of downtown, shifting much of the hotel, restaurant, and retail trade away from Whitehall Street.

also worked to transform the spatial and residential layout of Atlanta. The railroads were the reason for Atlanta's founding and spurred the growth of the city both before and after the Civil War. Even as late as the 1920s, they remained the city's foremost employer, pumping an estimated $100 million a year into the local economy. The railroads also transported products and people to and from Atlanta, securing the city's position and reputation as a major regional transportation center. Rail lines such as Seaboard Air-Line (between Birmingham and Atlanta) and the Louisville and Nashville linked up with the city during this period and increased both Atlanta's passenger and freight loads. New and impressive railroad stations were built to handle these increasing loads—Terminal Station in 1905 and Union Station in 1930. By 1927, some 326 passenger trains alone were passing through Atlanta each day.

The No. 2 trolley line, riding along Ponce de Leon through Druid Hills. Designed in 1893, Druid Hills was Frederick Law Olmsted's last suburb, though it was not actually developed until the early 1900s.

STREETCAR SUBURBS — Yet as important as railroads were to Atlanta's economy and growth during the first half of the twentieth century, it was the newer and emerging forms of public transportation, such as the electric streetcars, automobiles, and airplanes, that would have the greatest impact on the city's layout and future development. The emergence of electric streetcars and streetcar lines in the late nineteenth and early twentieth century, for example, was responsible for spurring the development of the city's earliest suburban communities. Joel Hurt, a civil engineer and realtor, played a prominent role in this development, helping to found not only the Atlanta and Edgewood Street Railroad Company in 1886 but also the East Atlanta Land Company, which laid out, promoted, and constructed Inman Park—the city's first planned suburban community. A number of the city's elite, including Asa Candler, lived in Inman Park and commuted to the city via the streetcar line that Hurt's company had constructed along Edgewood Avenue. Other streetcar lines served the emerging elite communities of Druid Hills (designed by famed landscape architect Frederick Law Olmsted) and Ansley Park. By 1913, the city's extensive streetcar system, owned and operated by Georgia Railway and Power Company (later Georgia Power), was carrying over fifty-seven million passengers a year and served not only upper-class suburban communities, but also working-class neighborhoods, industrial and commercial sectors, and the city's expanding parks and recreational areas. For most of Atlanta's population during these early decades of the twentieth century, the streetcar was the essence of public transportation.

THE AUTOMOBILE — Another form of transportation was already emerging, however, that would challenge and eventually supplant the streetcar as the preferred means of public transportation—the automobile. It was the automobile as well that did the most to hasten the move to the suburbs and redraw Atlanta's residential "color line." By the 1930s, two major population shifts were evident in the metropolitan area: a movement of middle- and upper-class white Atlantans to the north side of town and a migration of black Atlantans from the east to the west side.

Peachtree Street as it looked at the beginning of the twentieth century, when it was home to white elites, before commercialization and transportation improvements (particularly the automobile) spurred a northward migration into the emerging suburbs.

To fully understand the impact of the automobile on Atlanta, it is necessary to look back at what the city was like at the turn of the century. Henry Grady, the city's most fervid and accomplished booster, described Atlanta as a "Northern city in the South" and suggested that the city was on an equal footing with New York and Chicago. At the turn of the century, however, Atlanta was clearly at an earlier stage of development than the industrial metropolises of New York, Chicago, or Boston. This was evident in both the city's size and its physical layout. In 1903, Atlanta's eleven-square-mile land area was about one-quarter the size of Boston's and one-thirtieth the size of New York's. The city still had a circumferential shape—the same size and shape as Boston had in 1850. In addition, despite the influence of the railroads and streetcars, Atlanta was still, in many ways, a pedestrian or walking city, and as evidence of this, city administrators continued to pay far more attention to the construction and maintenance of sidewalks than they did to the paving of streets. In fact, before 1905 there were actually more paved sidewalks in Atlanta than paved streets, as almost 70 percent of the city's two hundred miles of streets remained unpaved. (By way of contrast, 30 percent of New York City's streets were unpaved and just 2 percent of Boston's.)

The presence of the automobile, however, began to change all this. Bicycle dealer William D. Alexander appears to have been the first Atlantan to own and operate an automobile. In 1901 he purchased and had sent to Atlanta three primitive 650-pound steam-driven Locomobiles. The cars had to be assembled upon arrival and operated without lamp, top, or horn. For the most part, they resembled carriages with wheels and were propelled by a steam engine mounted to the axle. Alexander's maiden nine-mile journey took two hours to complete, but despite the slow speed and primitive design of the vehicle, the automobile was clearly in Atlanta to stay. Within eight years, there were thirty-five car dealerships in the city offering customers a wide range of selections, including Pierce-Arrow, Premier, Cartercar, Maxwell, Hupmobile, Silent Selden, Hudson, Stearns, Pullman, Lambert, and Ford. From 1917 to 1926 Atlantans could also purchase a Hanson Six, which was produced locally by former wholesale grocer George W. Hanson and sold for $1,000.

The presence of the automobile in Atlanta added greatly to the traffic congestion and safety problems in the city. As noted earlier, a great number of trains made their way daily into and through Atlanta's central business district. These trains brought not only passengers and freight but also noise and pollution, and grade-level crossings, where city streets met rail lines, proved to be increasingly dangerous and congested areas. When the automobile was added to the mix, traffic and safety problems became even more acute, and Atlanta leaders began entertaining the idea of constructing a series of viaducts to bridge the noisy and dangerous downtown railroad chasm.

In 1909 the Atlanta Aldermanic Board and the Chamber of

The two-story city: a train stops beneath the Spring Street viaduct in 1942 while regular street traffic moves above it.

Commerce brought up the possibility of hiding the unsightly railroad lines by constructing a long axial mall some forty feet above the tracks where shoppers and workers could stroll along a pedestrian concourse flanked by palatial buildings. A similar (but even more elaborate) scheme was presented to the city seven years later by a New York engineering firm, but neither this nor the earlier "Bleckley Plan" (designed by local architect Haralson Bleckley) ever got off the drawing board. Once the automobile began to make its presence felt in downtown Atlanta, however, congestion increased, as did the pressure to do something about it, and in 1917 Mayor Asa Candler attempted to gain the support of the various railroads and property owners for the construction of a system of viaducts over the tracks. Four years passed before the city finally approved the plan through passage of a bond referendum. Construction of Atlanta's first viaduct for nonpedestrian traffic began in late 1921, and two years later the Spring Street viaduct, which linked Spring Street on the south with Madison Avenue on the north, was completed. It would take five more years, another bond referendum, and contributions from the railroads and Georgia Power totaling about $1.25 million before the Pryor Street and Central Avenue viaducts would be completed with lateral viaduct connections to Hunter Street (now Martin Luther King Jr. Drive), Alabama Street, and Wall Street.

The impact of the automobile not only spurred the elevation of the city's downtown, but also influenced the dispersal of Atlanta's population into the city's suburbs. As Atlantans in the mid-1920s began to seek suburban retreats farther away from the center of the city (and from the reaches of existing street-railway tracks), the motor vehicle increasingly became the preferred means of transportation. By 1930 the electric streetcar had fallen victim to the more flexible and convenient automobile and bus, and expanded (and paved) roads were beginning to link the suburban hinterlands with the central city and Atlanta with other cities in the state and region.

One of the most dramatic changes wrought by the appearance of the automobile was a suburban real estate boom that completely restructured Atlanta's residential patterns. Before the automobile, Atlanta's residential neighborhoods were highly centralized. Between 1910 and 1930, however, increased commercialization in the downtown area, a growing population, and a severe housing shortage generated a demand among the middle class for decentralized housing in less congested areas outside the city limits. The result was suburban residential expansion and the construction of a ring of bungalow-style houses (one-story structures that usually featured five to eight rooms on modest lots) surrounding Atlanta in a perimeter two to five miles from downtown. Included in this ring were Home Park and Virginia-Highland to the north; Candler Park/Edgewood to the east; Sylvan Hills and West End on the south; and Washington Park to the west.

The arrival of the automobile also brought about a dramatic shift in the residential distribution of Atlanta's white elite. In 1900, Atlanta's white, upper-class families lived within a few

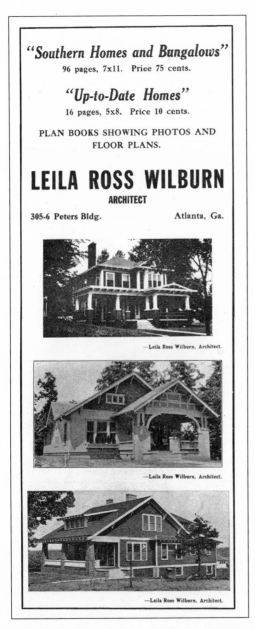

"Southern Homes and Bungalows"
96 pages, 7x11. Price 75 cents.

"Up-to-Date Homes"
16 pages, 5x8. Price 10 cents.

PLAN BOOKS SHOWING PHOTOS AND
FLOOR PLANS.

LEILA ROSS WILBURN

ARCHITECT

305-6 Peters Bldg.   Atlanta, Ga.

—Leila Ross Wilburn, Architect.

—Leila Ross Wilburn, Architect.

—Leila Ross Wilburn, Architect.

The spread of bungalow suburbs in Atlanta owes much to one of the city's first female architects, Leila Ross Wilburn, whose plan books were adopted by many local builders.

blocks of the city's financial and cultural institutions in the center of the city. Between 1910 and 1930, however, these families began to move farther north. By 1930, approximately 47 percent of Atlantans listed in the *Social Register* lived north of Ansley Park. This northward trek also greatly contributed to the growth of the Buckhead community, which grew from a population of 2,603 in 1920 to 10,356 ten years later.

On the other side of the color line, some suburbanization also occurred, particularly on the west side, where Heman Perry (founder of the Service Realty Company and a dozen related corporations that purchased, subdivided, and sold undeveloped land; provided financing for homeowners; and constructed houses) developed the black residential community of Washington Park. Despite the success of this project, which helped establish the west side of Atlanta as an area for black residential growth and expansion following World War II, suburbanization in Atlanta during this period remained, for the most part, "lily white." As a result, geographical distance was now added to the firmly entrenched Jim Crow patterns within the metropolitan area. Racial distance and separation in Atlanta was now not only political and social, it was increasingly spatial as well.

THE AIRPLANE — The automobile was not the only new mode of transportation that had an impact on Atlanta during the first half of the twentieth century. The airplane made its appearance in the city in the 1920s, and by the end of the decade, Atlanta had an airfield, a terminal, air mail and passenger routes, and an early connection with the airline industry that would serve the city well in the future. The person most responsible for establishing this connection was a young

The city's first municipal airport facility, Candler Field, pictured in 1927 when it opened to plane traffic. Candler Field is now Hartsfield International Airport.

city councilman and a later longtime mayor of Atlanta, William B. Hartsfield.

Hartsfield was elected to the Atlanta City Council in 1922 and was named chair of the council's aviation committee the following year. At that time, the informal center of the city's limited aviation activities was Candler Field, which featured a two-mile auto speedway and racetrack. In 1925 Asa Candler offered the city a five-year lease on the field in return for a waiver of property taxes, and after Hartsfield, at the urging of Mayor Walter Sims, surveyed the site and other potential airfield locations around the city (by air and by car), the city agreed to the proposal. While many Atlantans considered this expenditure a folly, Hartsfield recognized the potential value of establishing Atlanta as a regional center of aviation, and he played an instrumental role in securing the selection of Atlanta in 1928 as the southern terminal for an air mail route from New York to the Southeast and as a drop-off point for a national east-west air mail route two years later. In 1929 the city purchased Candler Field for $94,500, and within a year Pittcairn Aviation (the forerunner of Eastern Airlines) was making both mail and passenger runs out of Atlanta Municipal Airport at Candler Field.

The growing connection between Atlanta and the emerging aviation industry continued in the 1930s. In 1931, for example, the city opened America's first air passenger terminal, and seven years later it built the nation's first air traffic control tower. Once William B. Hartsfield became mayor in 1936 (a post he would hold for twenty-four of the next twenty-six years), the city's importance as a regional air center was established. (Atlanta's Hartsfield International Airport, today one of the busiest and largest airports in the world, is fittingly named in his honor.)

By the eve of World War II, Atlanta was the center of an impressive network of rail and air lines. The construction of a highway link to Savannah in 1935 and Georgia's first "superhighway" running between Atlanta and Marietta in 1938 was also establishing the city's importance as a regional trucking center. In the decades to follow, these transportation links would expand and grow in importance as Atlanta established its pre-eminent position as the transportation capital of the Southeast.

THE GREAT DEPRESSION

LOCAL RELIEF PROGRAMS — The growth and prosperity that characterized Atlanta during the early decades of the twentieth century were curtailed by the severe economic depression that gripped the nation in the 1930s. And like many cities in the South, Atlanta was poorly prepared to meet the emergency. In fact, Atlanta ranked last among similarly sized cities in 1930 in its per capita expenditures for welfare, and there were few municipal agencies or programs in place to help the rapidly growing number of unemployed. In 1932 thousands of hunger demonstrators marched on the Fulton County Courthouse to demand food and to protest a proposed plan by the county to slash its relief appropriations by one-third. Influenced by the turnout, the county commissioners instead voted to increase the relief budget by $6,000. Despite the increase, local relief efforts such as Fulton County's "self-help" program, which offered $1.25 toward groceries and a free lunch in return for work, and the Atlanta Chamber of Commerce's "back to the farm" project, which attempted to resettle the dispossessed on abandoned farms around the city, proved insufficient to meet the city's growing needs. By the spring of 1933, unemployment relief requests averaged over 12,000 per month with only $10.12 allocated for the average case, and by that summer approximately 60,000 Atlantans were already on the welfare roll.

NEW DEAL RELIEF AND EMPLOYMENT PROGRAMS — Some relief for unemployed and underemployed Atlantans during the early 1930s finally arrived with the inauguration of Franklin Delano Roosevelt as president and the institution of New Deal legislation and programs. In May 1933 the Roosevelt administration established the Federal Emergency Relief Administration (FERA), which was designed to provide both local relief and employment. Federal funds amounting to $3.3 billion became available to the city through this agency, and Atlanta mayor James Key quickly began getting agencies and plans in place to get the city and Fulton County's share. Georgia governor Eugene Talmadge, however, was vehemently opposed to Roosevelt and his programs and resented the amount of money allocated for Atlanta. (Talmadge's main source of political support was in the rural counties of Georgia, and his resentment toward Atlanta's

The Works Progress Administration, a federal agency, worked on Atlanta's sewers in the 1930s, bringing indoor plumbing to most of the city. Projects like these employed thousands of people and pumped millions of dollars into the local economy during the Great Depression.

power and influence was part of a continuing battle between the city and the rural politicians of the state.) Through his control of the Georgia Relief Commission, Talmadge held up relief work in Atlanta by refusing to help the city meet its part of the financial obligation. Harry Hopkins, director of the FERA, responded to the governor's resistance and interference by taking the Georgia Relief Commission out of Talmadge's hands and appointing Gay B. Shepparson as director of the state agency. As a result, Atlanta became one of the first cities in the nation to have a federally operated relief program, and under Shepparson's leadership FERA provided direct relief to the city, sponsored worker education classes at Atlanta University and elsewhere, set up public health services, and established work-relief projects.

New Deal programs and agencies that followed, such as the Civil Works Administration (CWA), the Public Works Administration (PWA), and the Works Progress Administration (WPA), pumped millions of additional dollars into Atlanta projects and employed thousands of city residents in the process. Projects undertaken by these agencies included the building or repair of area schools, hospitals, gymnasiums (including Georgia Tech's combination auditorium and gymnasium), and other public institutions; the grading of runways at Candler Field; the organization of a forty-five-member symphony orchestra; the repair and touch-up of the Cyclorama; and the construction of a new Atlanta sewer system. The new sewer system, which included 5.4 miles of trunk sewers and five sewage disposal plants and cost $11 million to construct, was a particularly significant improvement for the city. The old sewer system was inadequate and overburdened and had contributed, according to health officials, to Atlanta's leading the nation in diphtheria deaths in 1935 and a typhoid rate that was twice the average of the fifteen largest urban areas in the country.

PUBLIC HOUSING—The New Deal also spurred the construction of the nation's first public housing projects—Techwood Homes (for whites) and University Homes (for blacks). The idea for these projects had originated with Atlanta real estate developer Charles F. Palmer, who wished to rid the city of some of its slums

A kitchen unit in Techwood Homes, the first federally funded housing project in the country, completed in 1937 for whites only. Techwood, which was demolished to make way for Olympic housing, was paired with University Homes, a project near Atlanta University reserved for blacks only.

and replace them with federally funded public housing. Accordingly, Palmer selected a site (just south of Georgia Tech) where both blacks and whites were living in substandard housing, drew up plans and budgets for his proposed project, and began lobbying in Washington, D.C., for funding. Palmer also began a collaborative effort with John Hope, president of Atlanta University, who was desirous of developing additional housing for black Atlantans near the university.

Not everyone initially saw the wisdom of Palmer and Hope's proposal. Many local realtors and developers opposed the idea, and Washington dragged its feet when it came time to approve and fund the project. Others criticized public housing as being communistic and dangerous. Finally, however, Palmer got his way, and Roosevelt himself attended the dedication of Techwood Homes in the fall of 1936. Techwood opened its doors to its first residents the next year, and University Homes followed suit in 1938.

TENSIONS — The charges of communism surrounding Palmer's public housing proposal reflected a common concern of local officials and police that the economic distress of the Depression might lead to a communist insurrection and increased calls for black political, economic, and social equality. A small group of communists were present in the city during this period, and they did make efforts to organize both black and white workers. Their efforts were undermined, however, by the police, who frequently raided gatherings of communists, pacifists, and other groups that met on an interracial basis, arresting participants and charging them with violation of an 1866 state anti-insurrection law. These activities led the American Civil Liberties Union in 1937 to label Atlanta one of the nation's ten worst centers of repression.

One of the people arrested and jailed in these raids was Angelo Herndon, a nineteen-year-old black communist who had come to Atlanta to organize the unemployed. Herndon was charged with trying to overthrow the government and went on trial before a packed Atlanta courthouse in 1932. The jury found him guilty of the crime and recommended a sentence of eighteen to twenty years in prison. Herndon's arrest and conviction was challenged and publicized by the Communist Party, the International Labor Defense, and the Provisional Committee for the Defense of Angelo Herndon, and the case soon became an international *cause célèbre* and a symbol (much like the famous Scottsboro Boys case) of southern injustice. Finally, in 1937 the U.S. Supreme Court ruled that Georgia's anti-insurrection law was too vague, and Herndon and others arrested under this statute were eventually freed.

The economic and social tensions associated with the Depression also led to the emergence of several white supremacist organizations, including the American Order of Fascisti, or "Black Shirts," as they were commonly known. The Black Shirts grew quickly in number during the early 1930s and undertook a campaign to pressure Atlanta employers to fire their black workers and replace them with unemployed whites. Many employers complied with the organization's demands, but weaknesses within the movement (including the lack of a developed organizational structure and the absence of any program beyond a simple demand for white employment) soon led to its downfall.

As the rise of the Black Shirts suggests, employment opportunities for African Americans in Atlanta during the 1930s were severely restricted. Nevertheless, black workers in the city were not systematically excluded from federal programs as they frequently were in the state's rural areas. In fact, Mayor Hartsfield went so far as to veto a city council resolution that proposed that only white Atlantans be eligible for jobs on the city's WPA-funded sewer construction project. Still, services to the black communities of Atlanta were in no way equivalent to those offered whites. In May 1935, for example, the average general relief was $32.66 per month for whites versus $19.29 for African Americans.

By the late 1930s, the severity of the Depression in Atlanta was beginning to lessen. Private business was picking up, the federal government trimmed the number of WPA workers in the city, the banks were all back in operation, and aviation continued to be a growth industry. It would take World War II and the industrial development and expenditures associated with that effort, however, to fully return Atlanta to its earlier prosperity and launch the city into a new era of growth and transformation.

Atlanta
A Suburban Metropolis, 1940–1996

The '60s was the right time. Atlanta was the right city and this business community was the right one. No city has ever seen anything like it before and no city is likely to see it again.

—Ivan Allen, Jr., former mayor of Atlanta, 1980

s Atlanta neared the mid-century mark, the city again experienced a dramatic period of growth and change. New Deal public works and relief programs in the 1930s had helped rebuild the city's failing infrastructure and had eased somewhat the toll of the Depression on its citizens. But few industries, save the city's aviation-related businesses, experienced much growth during the decade. As the Depression came to a close, however, and America entered World War II, the local economy again began to pick up, the city's population increased, and Atlanta embarked on a period of impressive and sustained growth. In the decades following World War II, the city borders would expand through annexation and settlement in surrounding unincorporated counties; its air and rail connections would be augmented by important links to the nation's emerging interstate

Atlanta's downtown skyline continues to change; only one high-rise tower was built between 1930 and 1960; the real growth has occurred since 1960.

highway system; its central core would be reshaped through highway construction and urban renewal programs; and the arrival of professional sports teams, the growth and maturation of Atlanta's cultural arts, and the vertical expansion of the city's skyline through the addition of modern skyscrapers would add to Atlanta's emerging image as a "big league" city. In the process of all this growth and expansion, the city's economic, political, spatial, and racial structure was dramatically altered, and Atlanta became, in all senses of the word, a "metropolis"—the main city or capital of its region—and an urban center of growing national and international prominence.

WORLD WAR II

The second world war was a watershed event for the South in general and Atlanta in particular. Between 1940 and 1945, the federal government invested over $10 billion in war industries and military bases located in the South. It expended millions more on related projects such as public housing, health-care facilities, and aid to schools in the communities where the military buildup was the greatest. The addition of a million new civilian jobs region-wide through government projects and war industries helped curb high unemployment rates and sent wages and per capita income soaring in those areas where the industries and bases were located. The enlistment of large numbers of southern men and women into the armed forces (nearly one-third of the eleven million white men, more than two-thirds of the one million black men, and a high percentage of the quarter-million women who served in uniform were from the South) increased unemployment opportunities at home and spurred an exodus of rural southerners to cities in the South and North in search of good wages and more stable incomes.

World War II had an equally dramatic impact on Atlanta. It ended the Depression; swelled the city's population; spread a broad net of federal installations throughout the metropolitan area; enlisted blacks and whites, men and women, in the armed forces and in war-related industries; and brought to the forefront forces that would dramatically affect the city's race relations and politics in the post–World War II era. For better and worse, Atlanta would never be the same again.

THE MILITARY PRESENCE — Atlanta's most obvious connection to World War II was through the many military bases and support institutions that ringed the city. Camp Gordon, an army training base during World War I, was located along Peachtree Road in suburban northeast Atlanta and became the site during the second world war of a naval air base and Lawson General Hospital—a large medical complex that treated some 33,000 army personnel and war casualties during the period from 1941 to 1945. Fort McPherson in southwest Atlanta, which had served as a federal military barracks following the Civil War and as a training camp during World War I, was enlarged during World War II and utilized as an induction center. And the Atlanta General Depot (later Fort Gillem), an enormous army supply depot, was constructed on a 1,500-acre tract of land in Clayton County about fifteen miles southeast of downtown Atlanta. Also present in the metropolitan area was an army airfield, located (since 1929) adjacent to the city's municipal airport.

The clustering of these bases, supply depots, and military airfields in Atlanta, coupled with the city's traditional role as a railroad transportation center, meant that thousands of soldiers and military support personnel passed through or were stationed in Atlanta during the war, and their presence had both immediate and far-ranging consequences for the city. Soldiers from Fort McPherson, most of whom were white, and from Fort Benning in Columbus, Georgia, most of whom were black, frequently came to the city in search of entertainment and recreation, and Atlanta welcomed both groups—although on a segregated basis. Black soldiers passed through a separate "colored" entrance when they arrived in Atlanta at Terminal Station, and their activities, while they were in the city, were confined primarily to black-owned or -operated institutions. Representatives of the black U.S.O. or Traveler's Aid greeted the visitors at the railroad station and directed them to the Butler Street YMCA, where they could play basketball, ping pong, or checkers, swim, or attend dances, or to nearby Auburn Avenue, where a wide spectrum of black businesses, restaurants, nightclubs, hotels, and social activities were available to the visiting servicemen and women. When the Butler Street YMCA became too crowded, a U.S.O. unit was established at Booker T. Washington High School. Facilities and recreational opportunities for white soldiers were more widespread throughout the city, but essentially they provided the same services as those in Atlanta's black communities. Unlike black businesses, however, which occasionally served white servicemen, these white facilities were strictly off-limits to black soldiers.

As might be expected, Atlanta's entertainment and service industries, both black and white, benefited from the presence of the military population. But the impact of the military buildup in the city had its negative effects as well. Housing was increasingly in short supply, as building materials were reserved for military projects and housing construction in Atlanta ground to a halt. The conservation of materials for the war effort also led to a rationing among the civilian population in Atlanta (as elsewhere in the nation) of scarce items such as meat, sugar, coffee, tires, and gasoline. And finally, the presence of large numbers of soldiers on leave in the city led, on occasion, to disturbances of the peace and contributed to a near epidemic outbreak of venereal disease in Atlanta. To combat these problems, black and white military police (M.P.'s) patrolled the city's entertainment districts, and local officials clamped down hard on violators of the city's moral codes. (It was against the law in Atlanta, for example, for an unmarried man and woman to be alone together in a room with the door closed.) These actions, coupled with the widespread availability of penicillin (which the government dispensed for free), eventually helped bring venereal disease rates under control.

WAR INDUSTRIES — On a more positive note, the preparations for war also spurred the growth of war-related industries within the Atlanta metropolitan area and offered increased employment opportunities for the city's residents. Chevrolet's Lakewood

The Bell Aircraft bomber plant in Marietta, the largest war industry in metro-politan Atlanta, employed thirty-thousand people, 45 percent of them women.

plant, for example, converted its operations during the war to the production of munitions. The largest war industry to locate in the area, however, was Bell Aircraft (forerunner of Lockheed), which built B-29 bombers for use in the war. At its peak, the Bell plant, which was located in Marietta, employed about thirty-thousand workers, including a sizable number of women and a growing number of African Americans.

The inclusion of these two groups in the workforce was primarily the result of an increasing shortage of employable white males (due to the induction of most able-bodied men into the armed forces) and President Franklin Roosevelt's issuance in 1941 of Executive Order 8802, which outlawed racial discrimination in defense plants. As white women moved into defense work and received promotions, and as more and more African American men were drafted into the military, positions began to open up in the defense plants for black women. For the most part, however, these openings were confined to the lower-paying, more menial positions. Nonetheless, an important precedent had been set. For one of the first times in the city's history, blacks and whites, males and females, were working together in an industrial setting.

COCA-COLA GOES TO WAR — Another famous Atlanta company—Coca-Cola—also became involved in the war and, in fact, ended up accompanying the servicemen overseas. When Coca-Cola realized that sugar rationing would be extended to soft drinks, the company successfully lobbied to exclude the military from

During World War II, Coca-Cola followed American soldiers onto three foreign continents, popularizing the soft drink around the world.

rationing and then obtained the soft drink contract with the armed forces. Bottling plants, which were technically under the supervision of the military, were established at numerous locations overseas, and Coca-Cola literally followed the servicemen onto three continents. Technicians were sent out to the various plants to make sure that the product remained consistent, and portable backpacks that could dispense the soft drink were even carried to the front lines. In the process, Coca-Cola not only became a favorite drink among American GIs, but increased its international presence and influence as well. By the end of the war, Coca-Cola was well poised to further expand its production and distribution throughout the world.

THE USS *ATLANTA* — Atlanta's support for the war extended beyond the involvement of local industries and companies in the war effort and the induction of many of its young men into the service. Atlanta's civilian population also supported the war effort through participation in volunteer organizations like the Red Cross and the Civilian Defense and through the purchasing of war bonds. The greatest single indicator of Atlanta's commitment to the war effort, however, may have been the city's incredibly successful campaign to underwrite the cost of building a new navy warship.

The USS *Atlanta*, a naval cruiser, had been christened by Margaret Mitchell (author of the novel *Gone with the Wind*) and launched into action on September 6, 1941. In November 1942, the ship was torpedoed and sunk off Guadalcanal. Mayor Hartsfield spearheaded a war bond drive in Atlanta to raise the necessary funds to replace the ship, and the campaign succeeded in collecting almost enough money to build two ships. On February 6, 1944, a second USS *Atlanta* was christened (again by Margaret Mitchell) and sent into action. After engagements in the Far East theater, the ship was decommissioned on July 1, 1949, and placed in the Pacific Reserve Fleet. (It was later sunk during an explosives test off San Clemente Island, California, in 1970.) The first *Atlanta* earned five battle stars for her service during World War II; the second ship was awarded two battle stars for her accomplishments during the war.

When the naval cruiser USS Atlanta *was sunk off Guadalcanal in 1942, Atlantans raised more than enough money to replace the ship.*

FIGHTING FOR DEMOCRACY AT HOME — Although there was widespread support for the war in Atlanta, the experiences of some soldiers, especially black veterans, caused them to rethink and to challenge the assumptions and restrictions of Jim Crow. Southern blacks who served in the war resented the fact that they were being asked to risk their lives to fight racism abroad at the same time that they remained segregated and discriminated against in the armed forces and at home. The black press seized on this issue during the war and emphasized to its readers time and time again the importance of fighting a two-front war for democracy at home and abroad.

And black veterans were not the only southerners whose traditional views of race and race relations were challenged during the war. Harold C. Fleming, a young white Georgian who served as a company commander of black soldiers in World War II, became aware of the injustices of Jim Crow as a result of his wartime experiences. "It did more to change my life," he later related, "than any other experience I've ever had." When he returned to Georgia in 1947, Fleming moved to Atlanta where he became involved in and later served as executive director of an organization dedicated to fighting racial discrimination—the Southern Regional Council.

The Southern Regional Council was born on August 5, 1943, at a meeting held at Atlanta University. Here, an interracial group of prominent black and white leaders (including Ralph McGill, editor of the *Atlanta Constitution*; Methodist bishop Arthur J. Moore;

Atlanta Constitution *editor Ralph McGill, known as the "conscience of the South" for his outspoken political views and criticism of racial conservatism.*

Benjamin Mays, president of Morehouse College; and Atlanta University president Rufus E. Clement) met to respond to a challenge issued by an earlier conference of black leaders that had met in Durham, North Carolina. The signers of the "Durham Manifesto," as it came to be known, had declared that they were "fundamentally opposed to the principle and practice of compulsory segregation in our American society" and had further concluded "that it is possible to evolve in the South a way of life, consistent with the principles for which we as a nation are fighting throughout the world that will free us all, white and Negro alike, from want, and from throttling fears." The forty delegates who met in Atlanta concurred with these statements and resolved to create a "strong, unified Southern Regional Council" that, unlike its predecessor, the Commission on Interracial Cooperation (CIC), would include and involve African Americans on an equal basis with whites. Like the CIC and the Durham Manifesto, however, the council reluctantly agreed to postpone a direct attack upon segregation and concentrate instead on achieving "equal opportunity for all peoples of the region." On January 6, 1944, the Southern Regional Council was granted a charter and began what would be a long campaign to achieve racial justice and equality in Atlanta and throughout the South. Initially the council sought to improve race relations through programs of research and education and through behind-the-scenes negotiations and discussions with politicians and civic leaders promoting racial moderation. By 1951, however, the council's Board of Directors concluded that this course of action had not proven fruitful and endorsed instead racial desegregation as the organization's primary goal.

POSTWAR GROWTH AND EXPANSION

World War II in Atlanta had been a period of deprivation and shortages, but it was also an era of impressive growth for the metropolitan region and its industries. The postwar period continued and extended this growth. In 1947, a new Ford assembly plant was opened in Hapeville, and the following year, General Motors opened a new factory in Doraville. Bell Aircraft, the Atlanta area's biggest wartime industry, shut down in 1946 but reopened as Lockheed-Georgia only five years later (during the Korean conflict). By 1954 there were 800 new industries in Atlanta and almost 1,200 national corporations with offices in the city.

Margaret Mitchell Square in downtown Atlanta immediately after World War II.

ANNEXATION AND GOVERNMENT REORGANIZATION — Atlanta's civic and political leaders welcomed this growth and made efforts to support and sustain it through an aggressive annexation drive, urban renewal projects, and changes and improvements in the city's transportation systems, its water supply, and its government structure. The 1951 Plan of Improvement, drawn up by a citizens' study commission, brought about several of these changes. One of the major elements of the plan was a proposal to restructure the government responsibilities of the City of Atlanta and Fulton County to eliminate duplicate services. Under this plan, the city would take over park and recreation duties and police and fire protection, and the county would assume responsibility for health and welfare services and tax collection. In addition to these changes, the 1951 Plan of Improvement also called for the annexation of some densely populated areas north and south of the city. Similar annexation plans had been rejected in 1938, 1943, and 1947, but this time the referendum passed. As a result, the size of the city tripled in 1952 from 37 to 118 square miles, and almost 100,000 new residents were added to the city's population, bringing the total to 428,299.

HIGHWAYS AND AIRWAYS — Important changes were also brought about in the city's highways and airways. In 1946 (some ten years before the federal interstate highway program was established), white business leaders in Atlanta pushed for the adoption of the so-called Lochner report—a plan prepared by national traffic consultant H. W. Lochner that called for, among other things, the construction of a north-south expressway through downtown Atlanta. City voters approved a $16 million bond campaign to begin buying the right-of-way, and in 1949, with assistance from the federal and state government, the highway construction project was begun. By 1956, when the federal government launched its national interstate highway construction project (providing 90 percent of the necessary funding), the Atlanta expressway was already handling levels of traffic projected for 1970. Atlanta's early preparedness allowed the city to eventually link up with three major interstate highways (I-75, I-85, and I-20) and to construct an outer-ring expressway (I-285) to encircle the city and provide connections between the major transportation arteries.

Air traffic also continued to be an important growth industry in the postwar period, and Atlanta effectively strengthened and extended its connections in this field as well. Atlanta had pioneered several "firsts" in aviation. It was the first city, for example, to have an air traffic control tower (1938) and the first to utilize an instrument approach system (1942). This early commitment to the air industry, coupled with the expanded use of Atlanta's air facilities during World War II, put the city in a competitive position to capture regional control of air passenger service following the war. By the end of World War II, two major airlines, Eastern and Delta, were already headquartered in and operating out of the Atlanta municipal airport, and city hall, under the leadership of Mayor William Hartsfield, was committed to an expansion of the facilities and services offered at Candler Field. In 1948, Atlanta opened a new passenger terminal at the airport—a large metal, Quonset hut–style facility that cost the city $180,000 to construct. This was followed in 1961 by another brand-new terminal (which also proved obsolete within twenty years). By 1971, Hartsfield International Airport was already recognized as the second busiest terminal in the United States (Chicago's O'Hare was first) and the fourth busiest in the world.

CITY SERVICES — The remarkable growth and expansion that occurred in Atlanta during the postwar period also necessitated changes and improvements in the city's water systems, its public educational facilities, and its medical services. The first problem was addressed by the construction by the Army Corps of Engineers of Buford Dam in 1956. This dam, which had been enthusiastically supported by Mayor Hartsfield, Georgia senators Walter George and Richard Russell, and area congressmen, reserved enough water from the Chattahoochee River to supply two million Atlanta area residents and also created a very popular recreational lake with 540 miles of shoreline (Lake Lanier). Atlanta's public schools were also upgraded and expanded during this period, and the practice of sexually segregating the city's high schools was finally ended and replaced by a system of coeducational neighborhood schools. Racial segregation in the city's public schools did not end at this time, however, and remained strictly in force until 1961. Medical services and institutions in the city also grew during this period, although they remained segregated as well. In 1958, a new and expanded Grady Memorial Hospital opened under the aegis of the Fulton-DeKalb Hospital Authority. Black patients in the city, however, continued to be treated and hospitalized at the associated Hughes Spalding Pavilion.

The construction of the new Grady Hospital was a good example of the increased postwar cooperation among Atlanta's urban counties. Another indication of the recognized need for planning at the larger multicounty or metropolitan level was the establishment of the Metropolitan Planning Commission (MPC)

by Georgia's General Assembly in 1947. The MPC was originally a two-county planning body with authority to recommend
(but not enact) plans for the orderly growth and development of
the Atlanta metropolitan area. Later, the MPC would evolve into
the Atlanta Regional Commission (ARC), which oversaw a much
larger seven-county area (Fulton, DeKalb, Cobb, Clayton,
Gwinnett, Rockdale, and Douglas). Like its predecessor, however, the ARC would continue to function primarily as a regional
advisory board.

HOUSING AND URBAN RENEWAL — One of the first problem areas
that the Metropolitan Planning Commission tried to address was
Atlanta's pressing postwar housing shortage. The Depression of
the 1930s had slowed housing construction in the city, and building efforts during World War II had largely been reserved for war-
related projects. As a result, much of the city's housing supply was
overcrowded and deteriorating by the war's end.

The housing problem was particularly acute in Atlanta's black
communities, where overcrowding and structural deterioration
were typically at their worst. Despite the presence of a sizable and
growing black middle class, housing options for African Americans
in Atlanta were severely limited by a combination of forces including discriminatory lending practices, restrictive covenants and
deeds (private property restrictions written into deeds and neighborhood ordinances that declared certain neighborhoods off-limits
to African Americans and Jews), zoning regulations, terrorism and
violence, and strategically placed and strengthened barriers within
the city (such as industrial zones, railroads and highways, cemeter-
ies, and dead-end or unpaved streets), which served to divide whites
and blacks into separate neighborhoods. Except for the limited residential expansion that had occurred on the city's west side during
the 1920s and 1930s, Atlanta's black population was largely confined to older sections of the city surrounding the central business
district. By 1950, Auburn Avenue—the pride of black Atlanta, the
birthplace of Martin Luther King, Jr., and a showcase in the early
twentieth century for black business and residential wealth—contained over 25,000 persons per square mile. Black communities

also were burdened by aged and deteriorating housing. In 1950, for example, over two-thirds of the black dwelling units in the city, according to the U.S. census, were "dilapidated." (By way of contrast, only 14 percent of the white dwelling units were similarly classified.) Ten years later, almost three-fourths of all the dilapidated residential structures to be found in Atlanta were located in black communities.

The city's urban renewal programs and highway construction projects of the 1950s and 1960s threatened to make the situation even worse. The route of the north-south expressway, for example, bisected Auburn Avenue and wiped out areas of inner-city neighborhoods. Similarly, urban renewal projects, which resulted in the construction of a new civic center and a stadium, also destroyed homes and displaced residents in the process. In the period from 1956 to 1966 alone, almost 67,000 persons—the vast majority of them poor and black—were uprooted by these governmental activities. And while urban renewal programs eventually included provisions for the relocation of those displaced, only about 11 percent of the displacees who qualified for public housing during this ten-year period were actually relocated to public housing projects.

In response to this worsening housing problem, black leaders and organizations quickly mobilized to negotiate with city hall over replacement housing and agreed-upon areas for black residential expansion. In 1946, the same year that the Lochner report was released, the Atlanta Urban League called a meeting of representatives from business, government, and social agencies to discuss the issue. A Temporary Coordinating Committee on Housing was created with Walter H. Aiken, a leading black contractor, as chairman. The coordinating committee in turn established three other committees: a land committee, chaired by T. M. Alexander, a realtor, "to investigate further the possibility of getting outlet areas for Negro expansion"; a corporation committee, composed of representatives from Atlanta Mutual Building and Loan Association, the Atlanta Life Insurance Company, and Citizens Trust—to study the feasibility of setting up a corporation to build on the

Urban renewal and highway construction displaced 67,000 residents, most of them black, from downtown areas between 1956 and 1966.

selected sites; and a third committee, which was charged with working closely with and influencing county planners, the Atlanta Chamber of Commerce, and other governmental housing organizations and agencies.

In 1947 the coordinating and land committees enlarged their membership to include representatives from the Community Planning Council, the Empire Real Estate Board (of black realtors), and the land planning and racial relations units of the local Federal Housing Administration. This expanded committee, which became known as the Atlanta Housing Council, subsequently issued a report identifying six areas of Atlanta in which the committee felt the black population could and should expand. In each area, the report emphasized, some African Americans were already residing, and land (much of which was owned by African Americans) was readily available for residential development.

Although city officials had no public involvement in the housing council's deliberations, the Hartsfield administration privately endorsed both the general concept of black residential expansion areas and the specific sites suggested by the council. Five years later, the Metropolitan Planning Commission identified its own proposed black expansion areas in a document entitled *Up Ahead*. In this planning report, the commission acknowledged a "serious concentration of Negroes in unhealthy and inadequate downtown neighborhoods," resulting from the inability of blacks to secure either enough available used housing or enough open development land to meet the group's growing needs. The solution, according to the commission's report, was "to find outlying expansion areas to be developed for new colored housing." The document then went on to identify several possible expansion sites.

Up Ahead received severe criticism both from whites who owned land in the proposed expansion areas and from some African Americans who felt that the commission's plans would help to preserve and even intensify the already rigid residential segregation patterns within the metropolitan area. The immediate need of blacks for greater housing space, however, eventually overcame the objections of both groups, and by 1955 all six areas named by the Atlanta Housing Council as expansion areas in 1947 and four of those identified in *Up Ahead* had been developed as black residential communities.

Black leaders also succeeded in gaining new public housing for the poor in their communities. Carver Homes, for example, opened in 1953 on the south side, and Perry Homes opened two years later on the west side. By one account, some 1,990 new public housing units, 3,100 new private apartments, and 3,450 new owner-occupied homes were built for black residents in Atlanta during the period from 1945 to

1956. This new construction helped ease the housing shortage somewhat for black Atlantans, but it did little to end or diminish residential segregation in the city. Instead, new housing, including public housing, tended to be located in already existing black communities. As a result, public housing in Atlanta during this period tended not to disperse the black population throughout the metropolitan area, but instead to confine it to those areas of the city where African Americans were already present in sizable numbers.

THE GOVERNING COALITION

That Atlanta's black community could exercise any voice in the city's policies during the post–World War II period was testimony both to its growing political strength and William B. Hartsfield's political acumen and racial progressiveness. Early in his political career, Hartsfield had been a traditional southern segregationist. He had fought the creation of the Fair Employment Practices Commission in the 1930s and had even asked the House Un-American Activities Committee in 1944 to investigate the NAACP. Mayor Hartsfield, however, was no typical racial demagogue. As black political and economic power began to grow in the postwar period, Hartsfield realized that the black middle class could provide some much needed support for his reform-style politics. This black political support was essential to Hartsfield since he was losing much of his earlier political base with the exodus of educated and affluent whites to the Atlanta suburbs. After blacks marched on city hall demanding fairer law enforcement and the hiring of black police officers, Hartsfield met with leaders of the group to discuss the issue. This meeting set the precedent for what would become a Hartsfield administration trademark—quiet, behind-the-scenes negotiations with black leaders to resolve difficult racial issues.

Such meetings would never have happened, of course, if Atlanta African Americans had not managed in the 1940s to increase dramatically their percentage of the total city electorate.

The power structure: Mayor William Hartsfield listens to Robert W. Woodruff, "Mr. Anonymous" and head of Coca-Cola, whose philanthropy and business influence helped shape Atlanta politics and growth.

Several events and forces contributed to this increase. The repeal of the poll tax by the Georgia legislature in 1945 and the invalidation of the white primary by the U.S. Supreme Court the following year, for example, removed two very important barriers to black political participation in state and local elections. But the greatest impetus to increased black voter registration in Atlanta was a very successful and well-organized voter registration drive conducted and coordinated in 1946 by the All-Citizens Registration Committee (which included representatives of the NAACP, the Urban League, the Atlanta Civic and Political League, and other black political and civic organizations). As a result of this drive, almost 18,000 new black voters were added to the registration books in a period of only 51 days, and by the end of the year there were a total of 21,000 registered black voters in Atlanta. (By way of contrast, there were only about 3,000 registered black voters in 1945.) In 1949, in an effort to coordi-

Voter registrations undertaken by the All Citizens Registration Committee in 1946 added 18,000 African Americans to the rolls in 51 days.

nate and concentrate their new-found political strength, black Republicans and Democrats joined together to form the Atlanta Negro Voters' League—a body that was soon openly courted by the mayor and other white candidates for public office.

Despite their growing electoral strength, African Americans were still a minority partner at best in the governing coalition of Atlanta. Mayor Hartsfield recognized the importance of the black vote, but the greatest influence upon the policies of his administration came not from black leadership but from the leaders among the white business elite of Atlanta. These business leaders had played a large role in shaping city development and priorities during the first four decades of the twentieth century, but their influence within and upon city hall grew dramatically after World War II. Downtown merchants, businessmen, and major property owners formed the Central Atlanta Improvement

Association in 1941, and this group had a major role in developing and designing the highway construction and urban renewal programs that reshaped the city's core. They threw their support behind the Lochner plan, which proposed a route for the north-south expressway that would curve around the edge of downtown, forming a buffer between the business district and the black neighborhoods to the east, and they worked closely with the Metropolitan Planning Commission in laying plans to rejuvenate and expand the central business district. The downtown white business elite also endorsed, in general, urban renewal projects that would result in new public facilities (but not public housing) in the central city and favored the relocation of displaced black residents to outlying areas to the west and south.

The goals and objectives of the white business elite, however, did not always run counter to the wishes and interests of Atlanta's black community. In fact, the city's white business leaders, concerned about the image of Atlanta in national business circles, largely supported Hartsfield's and the black leadership's efforts to remove or weaken some of the most glaring inequalities under Jim Crow. And it was their support and influence that often proved crucial in later efforts to peacefully desegregate the city's public facilities.

CIVIL RIGHTS AND DESEGREGATION

Although African Americans continued to play a minor role in local governance until the 1970s, the growing political strength and influence of African Americans in postwar Atlanta was reflected in a number of areas. In 1946, black votes proved critical to the election of Helen Mankin Douglas as a congressional representative from the Fifth District. And in 1953, Atlanta University president Rufus Clement became the first African American to hold citywide office in the twentieth century when he was elected to the Atlanta school board. Negotiated settlements and behind-the-scenes discussions between black leaders and city hall also led to an easing of Jim Crow restrictions in some areas.

In return for black electoral support for the 1951 Plan of Improvement, for example, Mayor Hartsfield privately promised to help ease some of the more glaring and irritating symbols of racial segregation. Accordingly, he continued to reduce the size of "white" and "colored" signs at the Atlanta airport until the signs eventually disappeared. And in 1958, after long negotiations with key black ministers, the mayor helped stage a test case of state bus segregation laws. Similar laws in other states had already been declared by federal courts to be unconstitutional, and African Americans in Atlanta were anxious to challenge these statutes. A plan was thus worked out whereby a preselected group of black protesters would be arrested for violating state segregation laws. After their arrest, the protesters were immediately released on bond, the state law was declared unconstitutional, and Atlanta's buses were then integrated (sparing the city the long and costly demonstrations that had gripped Montgomery, Alabama, three years earlier). The desegregation of municipal golf courses was similarly negotiated behind the scenes and achieved with a minimum of unrest and publicity.

The most notable success in desegregation during Hartsfield's administration, however, was not the disappearance of "white" and "colored" signs in the city's airport terminal or the integration of its buses or golf courses. It was the widely publicized and peaceful desegregation of Atlanta's public school system in 1961. The local impetus for desegregation was a suit filed against the Atlanta school system by the NAACP in 1958. The black plaintiffs in this suit won their case, and the court ordered Atlanta to submit a desegregation plan by December 1959. Although Mayor Hartsfield and others advocated abiding by the decision, it was by no means certain at the time that this process could be carried out peacefully and without incident. The Supreme Court's 1954 decision in *Brown v. The Board of Education* that called for the desegregation of the nation's schools had been met with vociferous and, at times, violent protest in the South. Attempts to integrate public schools in Little Rock, Arkansas, and New Orleans had resulted in civil disturbances, and white political leaders throughout the region issued the call for "mas-

During a period of high racial and ethnic tensions, the Temple, a Jewish synagogue, was bombed on October 2, 1958. Here Rabbi Jacob Rothschild and Mayor William Hartsfield survey the damage.

sive resistance" to efforts to desegregate the South's institutions and submitted a wide spectrum of plans to resist, delay, or circumvent the edict of the Supreme Court. In Georgia, the state legislature had already passed a law that required that schools close before submitting to desegregation, and the Georgia Association of County Commissioners had gone on record as being opposed to "any race mixing in any Georgia schools anywhere, at any time, under any circumstances."

Even in Atlanta, the population was far from unified on the

issue of school desegregation. Local pro-segregation forces had coalesced into two distinct organizations—the Metropolitan Association for Segregated Education (MASE) and Georgians Unwilling to Surrender (GUTS)—and a large number of white Atlantans still preferred segregation to its alternative. But an increasing number of Atlanta citizens were also becoming concerned about the possibility of violence accompanying massive resistance and the long-term consequences of closing the city's public schools. In 1957, eighty white Atlanta Protestant ministers signed a "manifesto" that urged obedience to the law and called for the preservation of the public school system. (Two years later, 311 ministers signed a second similar manifesto.) Mothers of school-aged children, worried about the possibility of closing the city's schools, responded to the crisis by forming an organization called Help Our Public Education (HOPE), and the Atlanta Chamber of Commerce continued to hammer home the important lessons to be learned from the experiences of Little Rock and New Orleans. Eventually, the Atlanta Board of Aldermen, the business community, the *Atlanta Constitution*, the League of Women Voters, the Board of Education, the Georgia Education Association, and other local civic organizations all came together in opposition to the principles and goals of massive resistance.

The image-conscious Mayor Hartsfield and his allies in the business community not only wanted to avoid violence but to make the city look good in the process. Hartsfield had coined the description of Atlanta in the 1950s as the "city too busy to hate," and he was determined that Atlanta live up to this slogan. The governing coalition in Atlanta thus launched a campaign to prepare the city for peaceful desegregation of its schools in the fall of 1961. Statistics were prepared to show how costly (in economic terms) Little Rock's 1957 riots had been, and Jane Hammer (wife of the first director of the Metropolitan Planning Commission) chaired an organization called OASIS, or Organizations Assisting Schools in September, that was made up of all of the major local organizations that supported peaceful desegregation.

Despite the widespread nature and effectiveness of this campaign, it was by no means certain that school desegregation would occur without incident. Relations between the black community and white business leaders were already strained by an aggressive sit-in campaign launched by black college students in 1960 to desegregate downtown restaurants and other public facilities, and in December of the same year, the English Avenue Elementary School in Atlanta (a black public school) and a dozen nearby houses were severely damaged by a bomb explosion. The governing coalition was eventually able to negotiate a "cooling-off period" with the student demonstrators so that public school desegregation could go forward, but tensions remained high as

Local black college students launched sit-in campaigns to desegregate Atlanta restaurants and public facilities; several students were arrested on Forsyth Street on February 12, 1961, during a sit-in at Rich's department store.

segregationists and white supremacy organizations fanned the fires of local emotion and discontent.

In response to these perceived threats to public safety, the Atlanta police department initiated an elaborate surveillance program of racial agitators and white supremacy organizations like the Ku Klux Klan, and a law-and-order week was organized during which churches and synagogues offered special prayer meetings for peaceful desegregation. These extraordinary efforts proved successful, and on August 30, 1961, nine black students (chosen from a pool of 133 candidates) peacefully integrated four Atlanta public high schools—Brown, Henry Grady, Murphy, and Northside.

Hartsfield and his business allies made the most of this momentous occasion and all its public relations benefits. The huge press corps attending the event (including two hundred out-of-town reporters) was briefed in an elaborate pressroom set up at city hall, given a handbook prepared by OASIS, driven from school to school to witness the peaceful integration, offered a bus tour of the city, and treated to an integrated cocktail party at the Biltmore Hotel that evening. Hartsfield labeled the occasion Atlanta's "finest hour," and many in the city and throughout the nation agreed. President John F. Kennedy called a press conference to praise the city and urged other communities throughout the region and the nation "to look closely at what Atlanta has done and to meet their responsibility, as the officials of Atlanta and Georgia have done, with courage, tolerance and, above all, respect for the law." Most of the national news media in attendance also lauded the city for its accomplishment. In reality, the integration that the national press and local citizens witnessed was little more than token, but the significance of the event was nonetheless momentous. Atlanta had proved to itself and to the world that racial desegregation could be achieved peaceably, and in the process the city earned for itself a reputation for racial progressivism and moderation in a region that was known for neither.

The KKK and other white supremacist groups protested the Atlanta newspaper editorials in support of human rights in the early 1960s; Atlanta police kept them under close surveillance.

BIG LEAGUE CITY

The close alliance between private business and public government continued during the administration of Atlanta's next mayor—Ivan Allen, Jr. Allen was a businessman himself and the former president of the Atlanta Chamber of Commerce. While president of that organization, he had helped formulate a six-point plan for city progress that included the speeding up of expressway construction; increased urban renewal; the construction of a new civic center and stadium; the development of a rapid transit system; a continued plan of gradual but steady school desegregation; and a call for additional low-income housing. Mayor Allen made this six-point program the priority of his administration and the means by which he hoped to make Atlanta into a big league city with public facilities, an economy, sports and cultural offerings, and a public transportation system to match those of other national urban centers. Within ten years, all of the projects outlined by Allen had been implemented, but not without some attendant discord and a fundamental restructuring of the city's spatial and racial configuration.

FORWARD ATLANTA: PART II — One of the first efforts of Mayor Allen to promote Atlanta's potential and promise involved the reintroduction of the "Forward Atlanta" campaign, a national advertisement blitz that his father had successfully utilized during the 1920s to bring new industries and businesses to the city. The second Forward Atlanta campaign was launched in 1961 by the chamber of commerce and succeeded in raising $1.5 million from local businesses. These funds allowed the chamber to hire a professional staff, publish economic research data, and actively solicit new businesses through national advertisements that emphasized Atlanta's racial moderation, its pro-business environment, its prominence as a regional transportation and distribution center, and its beautiful homes and neighborhoods.

Like its predecessor, the second Forward Atlanta campaign succeeded in attracting new businesses to the city. For much of the early twentieth century, Atlanta had been a branch office town. In the 1960s it became a national headquarters city, as homegrown businesses attained national corporate status and other national businesses relocated to Atlanta. Job rolls expanded by tens of thousands each year during the decade, unemployment levels fell as low as 1.9 percent, and Atlanta continued to rank in the top ten cities in terms of downtown construction, bank clearings, and employment. The regional capital with aspirations of national prominence now had the businesses and the economic statistics to support its claims.

BIG LEAGUE SPORTS — One of the hallmarks of a "big league city" is the presence of major league sports teams, and in the 1960s Mayor Allen aggressively pursued his dream of bringing professional sports to Atlanta. In 1963 Allen met privately in Atlanta with Charles O. Finley, owner of the Kansas City Athletics of the American Baseball League. Finley offered to move his team to Atlanta if the city would build him a new stadium,

The Peachtree Road Race, a hot Independence Day run since 1970, has joined the ranks of national meets, especially the wheelchair division. In 1994 more than fifty-thousand people participated in the race.

and Allen agreed to the proposal. The site that the two men eventually agreed upon for the stadium was in an area to the immediate south of the central business district that had been cleared through an earlier urban renewal project. While the land at the time lay vacant, the city did not own the property (it was controlled by the Atlanta Housing Authority). Nevertheless, Allen went ahead with the plan. He met with Mills B. Lane, head of the Citizens and Southern Bank, and the two came up with a proposal to reconstitute the old Stadium Authority with Lane as treasurer and Coca-Cola Bottling Company executive Arthur Montgomery as chairman. Lane also agreed to pledge the full credit of his bank to the project.

While this plan was being put into effect, the American League informed the mayor that Finley did not have enough league votes to move his team to Atlanta. Arthur Montgomery received word, however, that stockholders of the Milwaukee Braves of the National Baseball League were interested in relocating their team, and a lunch meeting of Braves stockholders and Atlanta executives was arranged. A favorable response from the luncheon convinced Allen and his allies to continue with the project, and Mills Lane supplied money for architects to begin plans for the stadium even though there was not yet formal approval of the deal from the Braves, the city, or the county. As Mayor Allen later recounted, he and his friends were planning a stadium on "land we didn't own, with money we didn't have, for teams that didn't exist."

A handshake deal with the Milwaukee Braves representatives and their commitment that they would move the team to Atlanta in 1965 finally brought about the public announcement of the deal, and local government officials quickly swung into step to get the project under way and completed on time. The board of aldermen and the Fulton County Commission approved the plan, and the state legislative delegation from Atlanta rushed through the necessary authorization of the funding. To meet the tight construction deadline, the stadium authority agreed to pay an additional $600,000 premium to ensure that the stadium would be built within a year, and fifty-one weeks later the Atlanta–Fulton County Stadium was completed and ready for big league baseball.

Hank Aaron of the Atlanta Braves, baseball's all-time home-run king.

Ironically, the stadium had to wait an additional year for its new baseball team while the Milwaukee Braves were ensnarled in litigation with the City of Milwaukee. In the meantime, the stadium secured yet another tenant—a professional football team. As before, Allen relied upon the assistance of his business peers to bring off the deal, convincing Cox Broadcasting executive Leonard Reinsch that he should seek ownership of the new team. Reinsch concluded that the city's best bet would be to solicit the awarding of an American Football League franchise (since the National Football League had earlier turned the city down), and he succeeded in securing an AFL franchise contract. Before Reinsch could present his contract to the Stadium Authority, however, NFL commissioner Pete Rozelle changed his mind and decided that Atlanta would be a good market for an expansion team. As a result, Atlanta got a new NFL football team owned, not by Reinsch, but by insurance executive Rankin Smith, who had been introduced to Rozelle by Georgia governor Carl Sanders.

As a result of all these hurried and complex negotiations, Atlanta became the first city ever to obtain major-league baseball and foot-

*The Atlanta Falcons played their first game in Atlanta the year of their arrival,
1965.*

ball teams in a single year. The city also succeeded in adding a professional basketball team to its roster in 1968 when the St. Louis Hawks of the National Basketball Association relocated to Atlanta. At first, the Hawks played in Georgia Tech's Alexander Memorial Coliseum, but in 1972 they moved to a new home in the Omni, a $17 million entertainment and sports facility built on the old railroad gulch west of downtown. The first big league sports team to play in the new structure, however, was not the Hawks but the Atlanta Flames of the National Hockey League, who opened their inaugural season in the fall of 1972. (The team later moved to Calgary, Alberta, Canada, in 1980.)

THE "HIGH" ARTS — Arts and culture are another measure of urban prominence, and in the 1960s Atlanta cultural institutions grew in stature and in size. Unfortunately, their growth was spurred in large part by a tragic event. On June 3, 1962, 106 Atlantans, most of them members of the Atlanta Art Association, boarded a charter flight at the Orly airport in Paris, France. The members of the group, as Mayor Allen later described them, were "the backbone of Atlanta's cultural society, the city's leading patrons of the arts," and they were in the midst of a tour of European museums.

As the Air France 707 jet roared down the runway, something went wrong, and the pilot tried to abort the takeoff. The plane skidded off the end of the runway, plowed through a field, and crashed into a small stone cottage, where the jet burst into flames. All of the passengers on board were killed in the accident, and Atlanta's arts community was dealt a heavy blow.

Earlier in the year, Atlanta citizens had rejected a bond issue that included funding for an arts center in Piedmont Park. In the aftermath of the tragedy, however, $13 million was raised through private donations to build a new arts center dedicated to the memory of those who died at Orly. The Atlanta Memorial Arts Building (now the Robert W. Woodruff Arts Center) was completed in 1968 and initially housed not only the High Museum, but also the Atlanta Symphony Orchestra, the Atlanta College of Art, the Alliance Theatre, and the Atlanta Children's Theatre.

France donated a bronze cast of Rodin's L'Ombre *(The Shade) to Atlanta in memory of the 106 Atlantans killed in a plane crash at the Paris airport, June 3, 1962.*

Other cultural institutions that grew and matured during this period included the Center for Puppetry Arts, the Atlanta Ballet, and the Atlanta Historical Society (which moved its headquarters from Peachtree Street to the elegant Swan House in Buckhead in 1966).

MARTA — Another major element of Mayor Allen's six-point plan was the development of a rapid mass-transit system for the city and its surrounding environs, and in his second term of office, Allen succeeded in laying the foundations for the creation of the Metropolitan Atlanta Rapid Transit Authority (MARTA). The actual financing and startup of MARTA would not occur, however, until after Allen had retired.

The campaign for a modern transit system began in 1964 when voters approved an amendment to the state constitution that authorized the establishment of a regional transit authority and provided limited planning funds. A MARTA board was subsequently appointed to represent Atlanta and the surrounding suburban counties. In keeping with Atlanta's tradition of strong links between government and business, the city's representatives to the board consisted of four business executives—three whites (including department store owner Richard Rich, who became MARTA chairman) and one African American (L. D. Milton, president of Citizens Trust Company).

Despite this promising start, plans for MARTA and its rapid rail system quickly ran into difficulty. In 1968, Atlanta area voters rejected a proposal to underwrite the local cost of rail construction with property taxes. The measure was defeated not only in the suburban communities that took part in the election, but in the city as well, with Atlanta black voters comprising a significant portion of those opposed to the measure. Black leaders, including Jesse Hill (the president of Atlanta Life Insurance) criticized the project for excluding African Americans from the planning process, for neglecting to hire enough black workers, and for focusing too exclusively on the needs and wishes of white downtown interests.

Mayor Allen retired before these issues could be resolved, but his successor, Sam Massell, garnered the necessary votes to allow

MARTA to proceed with its plans. Before this could be achieved, however, MARTA had to go back to the drawing board and redesign both its proposed routes and its funding source. In place of a property tax increase, the Massell administration suggested a 1 percent sales tax to underwrite the local share of construction costs (the remaining amount would be picked up by the federal government). Even with these changes, opposition to the rapid transit system remained strong, especially among black voters, many of whom argued that the proposed sales tax was regressive and that it would hit the city's poor the hardest. Mayor Massell undercut this criticism to some extent by extracting a promise from the MARTA Board that it would set the fare for the system at fifteen cents and hold it there for seven years. In 1971 the proposal was submitted to the voters, and by a slender margin the referendum was approved.

OTHER MEASURES OF SUCCESS: POPULATION GROWTH, SHOPPING MALLS, OFFICE PARKS, AND TALL BUILDINGS — As the decade of the 1960s drew to a close, Mayor Allen saw many of his dreams for the city realized. Atlanta had a new stadium hosting big league baseball and football. A new civic center had been constructed on land cleared through urban renewal. The city had made itself the regional center of a rapidly expanding rail, air, and highway transportation system. The influx of new businesses and the growth of local ones had spurred the economy and made Atlanta the headquarters for many national corporations. And the city's many cultural arts institutions were growing, maturing, and becoming increasingly well known throughout the nation.

There were other indicators that Atlanta was becoming a major urban center. The metropolitan population, for example, reached the million mark in 1959, and continued to grow quickly during the following decade. The city's skyline was expanding as well. In the period from 1930 to 1960, only one high-rise building—the twenty-two-story Fulton National Bank building—was constructed in downtown Atlanta. In the 1960s, however, a number of new skyscrapers began to appear. One of the

John Portman's Merchandise Mart, the first building of Peachtree Center, a complex of shops, offices, and hotels that sparked skyscraper growth in downtown and moved the city center north of Five Points.

individuals most responsible for this trend was Atlanta architect John Portman. The first of Portman's downtown creations, the million-square-foot Merchandise Mart, was completed in 1961 and became the nucleus of a complex of office towers, hotels, retail shops, restaurants, and merchandise space known as Peachtree Center. Portman's innovative design features—such as his large open atriums (including the 20-story floor-to-roof atrium in the Hyatt Hotel)—dramatically influenced hotel architecture and were imitated throughout the United States and the world. Portman's success also spawned a flurry of construction in downtown Atlanta (17 skyscrapers of at least 15 floors were built during the 1960s) and helped pull the commercial center of the city farther north along Peachtree.

Growth and construction during this period was not just restricted to the downtown, however. In fact, the 1960s also saw the emergence of the city's earliest suburban malls and office parks. In 1959, Lenox Square, metropolitan Atlanta's first regional shopping center, opened in Buckhead, some seven miles north of the central business district. Richard Rich, the chief executive officer of Rich's department store, had made the decision to resist establishing any suburban stores until the interstate highway system was nearer completion and until the Atlanta metropolitan population reached the one million mark. When both of these conditions were met in 1959, Rich's became one of the anchor stores of Lenox Square and helped launch the beginnings of suburban mall development in the metropolitan area. By 1972 there were twenty-four major outlying shopping areas in the Atlanta region and eleven regional shopping centers.

While Atlanta may have lagged somewhat behind other cities in the construction of suburban retail centers, the city was a pioneer in the development of office parks. Between 1965 and 1971, new office parks in the Atlanta area accounted for the construction of over 5.2 million square feet of additional office space. Most of these new office parks were located in the northern suburbs of the city, where space for expansion was available and less costly and where an increasing percentage of the workforce (mostly white) now resided. Suburban industrial parks (which numbered over seventy by 1973) and trucking facilities, which were tied to the metro area's expanding freeway system, offered additional suburban employment and helped draw an increasing number of jobs and workers away from the central business district.

By 1970, despite a decade of impressive construction and development in downtown Atlanta, the city's suburbs were already outpacing the central city in population growth and housing construction. The city of Atlanta's population, for example, grew by less than 2 percent during the 1960s, and began to decline in numbers following its peak in 1970. The suburban population, on the other hand, mushroomed, accounting for over 86 percent of the total population increase in the Atlanta metropolitan area during the 1960s. Housing figures for this same period reflect a similar trend. In 1960, for example, housing within the city accounted for almost one-half of all the dwelling units in the metropolitan area. Ten years later, the city's share had fallen to 38 percent as dramatic suburban growth overshadowed inner-city housing construction, and the destruction of some thirty-four thousand homes within the city limits through urban renewal and highway construction contributed to yet another Atlanta housing shortage. From 1970 on, much of the impressive growth and development that would establish Atlanta as one of the nation's most important urban centers would take place in the expansive suburban regions beyond the city's borders.

RACE, POLITICS, AND CHANGES IN THE GOVERNING COALITION

At the same time that Atlanta was acquiring all the characteristics of a big league city, dramatic changes were also taking place in the makeup and goals of Atlanta's governing coalition. For much of the postwar period, city hall and the white business elite had been allied in a common cause to promote city growth and economic development. The black leadership of Atlanta had been content during this period to make use of their limited but well-coordinated political power and influence to negotiate the gradual relaxation of Jim Crow and to push for the desegregation of the city's public institutions. In the decade of the 1960s, however, a new leadership came to the fore in Atlanta's black communities—a leadership that was younger and less patient with the results and pace of the behind-the-scenes negotiations and "gentlemen's agreements" of the earlier era. By the end of the 1960s, the old biracial agreements were no longer in place, and African Americans had assumed control of the city's governing structure for the first time in Atlanta's history.

CRACKS IN THE COALITION — One of the first major challenges to the governing coalition occurred in 1961 when black college students organized sit-ins to desegregate Atlanta's downtown restaurants. This campaign, as noted earlier, threatened to upset relationships and alliances forged between black leaders and the white business elite and exposed generational cleavages within the black community. Martin Luther King, Jr., who had returned to Atlanta following the Montgomery bus boycott and who had personally participated in one of the sit-in demonstrations, soon found himself in the unenviable position of mediating between radical college students and older black leaders like his father, "Daddy" King, who favored a less confrontational approach. The younger Martin Luther King was able to bridge the generational divide and convince the student leaders to halt their protests in return for a promise from white business leaders that after a cooling-off period, the downtown stores would be desegregated. The coalition had held, but the cracks and divisions remained.

One year later, changes in black leadership and tactics became even more apparent in the response of African Americans to the so-called Peyton Road barricades. In that year, as blacks moved into the formerly whites-only subdivision of Peyton Forest in southwest Atlanta, the city responded, much as it had in the past, by erecting street barriers to slow and contain further black residential expansion. (Whites apparently continued to enter the subdivision from the south, where housing remained all white at the time.) The previous year, Mayor Hartsfield had put up a similar barricade in the same section of the city without much damaging reaction. This time, however, the response from the black community was quite different. Black leaders rejected newly elected Mayor Allen's offer to rezone 250 acres of nearby industrial land to allow the construction of low- to middle-income housing for African Americans and even declined his invitation to meet with representatives of the Atlanta Negro Voters League, the Empire Real Estate Board, and white homeowners to discuss the situation. The newly formed Citizens Committee for Better City Planning (which included representatives from new black organizations like the Southern Christian Leadership Conference [SCLC], the Student Non-Violent Coordinating Committee [SNCC], and the Committee on Appeal for Human Rights) kept up pressure on city hall to remove the barricades, and two suits were filed in court to challenge the city's actions.

In addition to the hostile reaction from Atlanta's black communities, the Peyton barricade episode attracted the attention of the national press in articles, reports, and editorials that questioned the city's racial progressivism and compared the barricade to the Berlin Wall. This publicity embarrassed the city and forced city hall to finally recognize that the days of a tightly segregated housing market in Atlanta, kept in place by overt discrimination and racial barriers, were now over. When a Fulton County Superior Court judge ruled that the barricade was unconstitutional, the mayor did not appeal the decision, but instead moved as quickly as possible to have the barriers taken down.

This public acknowledgment of the right of African Americans to housing on an equal opportunity basis was an important turning point in Atlanta's history. It paved the way for black residential expansion into new areas of the city (particularly in southwest Atlanta). It also accelerated the exodus of white Atlantans out of the city and into the suburbs. During the decade of the 1960s, the city's white population would decline by 60,000 while its black population increased by 70,000. Neighborhoods in southwest Atlanta were transformed, seemingly overnight, from all-white to majority-black communities. In the process, residential segregation within the city actually increased. In effect, the residential color line had finally been broken in Atlanta, only to be redrawn even more dramatically in the boundary between city and suburb.

Rabbi Rothschild and Dr. Martin Luther King, Jr., at the first formal, biracial, sit-down dinner in Atlanta, given to honor Dr. King's receipt of the Nobel Peace Prize, January 27, 1965.

In 1964, the city was presented with an opportunity to repair the strained relations between its black and white leaders when native son Martin Luther King, Jr., was presented with the Nobel Peace Prize. At first, the awarding of this prestigious honor presented Atlanta's white leadership with a dilemma. Some resented the role he had played in the sit-in campaign to desegregate downtown facilities and his involvement in other local protests (including labor union demonstrations at the Scripto Company factory). Still, to ignore the Nobel award would sully the city's national image and call into question its commitment to racial progress. King was honored in Washington and New York after his return to the United States, but when he arrived in Atlanta there was no official welcome from city hall. After persistent pressure and persuasion from Mayor Allen and Coca-Cola executive Robert W. Woodruff, however, the business community and its leadership reluctantly agreed to honor King with a biracial formal dinner (the first in the city's history), held at the Dinkler Hotel on January 27, 1965. More than fifteen hundred blacks and whites—including most of Atlanta's business leaders—attended the event.

In 1966, racial problems again surfaced in Atlanta when a riot broke out in Summerhill, a black community that Mayor Allen later described as "a tinderbox of poverty, disease, crime, frustration and unrest, sitting in the very shadow of our new stadium." The immediate cause of the unrest was the shooting and wounding of a black auto-theft suspect, but the underlying roots of the disturbance were unresolved complaints with city hall over neighborhood problems, including overcrowded housing, the absence of recreational facilities, and high unemployment. By five o'clock in the afternoon on the day the riot began, hundreds of protesting residents were in the streets. Mayor Allen arrived in the community along with some police and twenty-five black ministers whom he had summoned and tried to calm the crowd, but neither his nor the ministers' pleas were effective. Instead, as Allen got on top of a police car with a bullhorn to address the crowd, bricks were thrown, the car was rocked, and the mayor was forced to dive for safety into the arms of accompanying policemen. The crowd was finally dispersed with tear gas, and the unrest eventually subsided the following evening.

Less than one week later, racial violence again broke out—this time when a white man driving through the Boulevard area of the Bedford Pine community shot and killed a sixteen-year-old black youth. The incident set off a three-day riot in the area with police battling firebombs and bricks. About 20 people were injured and 140 arrested during this melee.

Initially, both the mayor and some of the media blamed the riots on the militant activities and agitating language of Stokely Carmichael and other members of the Student Non-Violent Coordinating Committee, who were present at both disturbances decrying police brutality and city neglect. But later, city hall came to accept the Council on Human Relations of Greater Atlanta's assessment that "the basic responsibility lies with Atlanta's lack of concern over miserable conditions in slum areas." Two months after the riots, Allen called a Mayor's Conference on Housing that set a two-year goal of 9,800 units of low- and moderate-income housing and a five-year goal of 16,800 units and set up a Community Relations Commission to hear complaints and recommendations of residents in low-income neighborhoods. Although the new housing goals were not met by the promised deadlines (due, in large part, to neighborhood factionalism and conflict, distrust of city officials, and disagreements over the location of subsidized housing), the dissatisfaction and unrest present in Atlanta's low-income black communities and violently expressed in these riots forced the city to reexamine and reshape its housing and urban renewal policies.

THE NEW POWER STRUCTURE — In April 1968, the city leadership again convened to honor Martin Luther King, Jr. This time, however, it was on the occasion of his assassination. More than 200,000 mourners (including well-known national politicians and celebrities) assembled in King's hometown to pay tribute to the great civil rights leader. And in the tradition of Atlanta's history of tragedy and rebirth, a commitment to black political progress emerged in the wake of King's death. Colleagues, as well as followers and admirers of King, turned to the ballot box to secure black political gains and representation, and they were successful.

In 1969, Maynard Jackson was elected as the city's first African American vice mayor (along with Sam Massell, the city's first Jewish mayor), and in 1972, Reverend Andrew Young (a colleague and aide of King) became the first black Georgian to be elected to Congress since Reconstruction. Black community representation in the Georgia legislature also increased during these years, and in 1973, Maynard Jackson became Atlanta's first African American mayor. That same year, blacks gained equal representation on the city council for the first time and a slight majority on the school board.

Another indication of the changing political climate in Atlanta in 1973 was the adoption of a new city charter that changed the selec-

Changes in the power structure: Sam Massell, Atlanta's first Jewish mayor (elected in 1969), with then–vice mayor Maynard Jackson, later Atlanta's first African American mayor (elected in 1973).

tion process for most city council members from at-large elections (which had traditionally been used to restrict minority representation) to district elections and that mandated the involvement of in-town neighborhoods in the preparation of one-, five-, and fifteen-year comprehensive development plans. That same year, a long-standing fight over city school desegregation was brought to a close by a negotiated settlement that, in effect, conferred black control over administrative and staff assignments in the school system and approved a student assignment plan that ensured that each city school would be at least 30 percent black. (In return for these assurances, the local NAACP dropped demands for busing and a metropolitan-wide end to racial imbalance in the schools.)

Maynard Jackson, Atlanta's new mayor, was sailing into unchartered governmental waters when he took office in 1974. Not only was Atlanta a majority black city for the first time in its history, but its charter had been fundamentally changed, and the old governing coalition that had ruled the city for decades was no longer in place. Jackson was in many ways, however, the perfect man for the job. Only thirty-five years of age when he was elected, Jackson was nonetheless very familiar with Atlanta, its politics, and its many economic, cultural, social, and political coalitions. Though born in Dallas, Texas, Maynard Jackson had strong Atlanta connections. His maternal grandfather was John Wesley Dobbs, a black community and fraternal leader who had championed voter registration in Atlanta (and who is credited with nicknaming Auburn Avenue "Sweet Auburn"), and his father was pastor of Atlanta's historic and influential Friendship Baptist Church from 1945 until his death in 1953.

Jackson's election signaled more than simply a racial change in the governing coalition of Atlanta. It also represented a fundamental transformation in the priorities and socio-economic makeup of local government itself. Before assuming office, Jackson announced his intention to create a new environment at city hall where "grass-roots leaders, white and black, will be sitting alongside of persons who are quite wealthy, quite influential, and sometimes not as attuned as they need to be to what it is really like to be living close to disaster." The new mayor hoped to bring new people and new groups to the bargaining table, and the composition and policies of his administration reflected that orientation. The number of women and minorities employed by the city shot up during Jackson's two terms in office, and his administration implemented a sweeping program to guarantee the black community and black businesses a substantial share of city business. Affirmative-action hiring policies were soon required of all city suppliers, and joint-venture arrangements were negotiated in situations where minority businesses were nonexistent or too small to handle the projects by themselves.

The new mayor's interest in involving grass-roots organizations in the government, planning, and development of the city was also reflected in the development of Atlanta's neighborhood planning unit (NPU) system. To carry out the new city charter's mandate for increased citizen participation, Atlanta was divided into twenty-four neighborhood planning units. Each unit was composed of a cluster of inner-city neighborhoods and was designed to bring together area community leaders and involve them in important decision-making processes. The new ordinance setting up the NPU system required that all planning and zoning proposals go before the affected NPUs for their reaction and comments, and Mayor Jackson created a Division of Neighborhood Planning to give the NPUs assistance in developing their priorities and in expressing their opinions.

These actions by the Jackson administration to involve grass-roots organizations in government and to increase participation by minority businesses in city projects alarmed and angered some members of Atlanta's white business elite. Particularly galling to these businessmen were Jackson's insistence that 20 percent of the contracts awarded to companies working on Atlanta's new $400 million airport go to minority firms, his suggestion that he might deposit the city's money in Birmingham banks if Atlanta's financial institutions did not name women and minorities to their boards and implement plans for members of these groups to progress up the corporate ladder, and his dramatic expansion of the powers and personnel of the mayor's office.

In response to these developments, Harold Brockey, the chairman of Central Atlanta Progress, an organization composed mainly of downtown business leaders and major property holders in the area, sent a letter to Mayor Jackson in which he outlined concerns about the lack of access to the mayor, the deterioration of the close historical relationship between business and government, and the growing perception within Atlanta's white business community that Jackson was antiwhite. When the local and national press caught wind of the letter and publicized it, both Jackson and white business leaders closed ranks to deny allegations that a rift was developing between the city and its white businesses and that these businessmen were making plans to abandon the city for the suburbs.

While the Brockey letter did not alter Maynard Jackson's priorities, it did lead to better communication between city hall and the business community. And in the process, Jackson and the white business elite succeeded in working out a set of accommodations that included an agreement that joint ventures would be encouraged, but not required, in airport construction contracts; the establishment of regular meetings between city hall and business leaders; the creation of an independent agency (the Atlanta Economic Development Corporation) to oversee and evaluate economic development projects; and Jackson's promise to make trips with members of the chamber of commerce to promote Atlanta and its investment potential. Jackson's election to office and the change in the racial composition of the city had forever transformed the local power structure, but biracial negotiations and cooperation were still an important part of Atlanta's governing style. Maynard Jackson's willingness to listen to and address business concerns and priorities ensured that these processes and the economic development of the region would continue to move forward.

Black control of the local political process was demonstrated anew in 1981, when Andrew Young defeated a well-financed white opponent, Sidney Marcus, in the race for mayor. Unlike Maynard Jackson, Andrew Young was already a well-known figure (both nationally and internationally) when he took office. He had been one of Martin Luther King, Jr.'s most trusted lieutenants during the civil rights movement, had been elected to Congress in 1972, and had served as President Jimmy Carter's ambassador to the United Nations. During his stint as U.N. ambassador, Young had earned the admiration of Third World nations and the criticism of some Western leaders and politicians for his sometimes unguarded and candid comments about the nature and priorities of Western diplomacy. Despite this reputation, Young was less an agitator than a conciliator. And it was during his administration as mayor that the relationship between city hall and the white business elite was strengthened and restored, and the power and influence of the neighborhood planning units was diminished.

Economic development was an important part of Andrew Young's plans for the city, and shortly after he took office he arranged a luncheon with downtown business leaders, most of whom had supported his opponent in the mayoral race. At this luncheon, Young opened his address to the businessmen by declaring that "I didn't get elected with your help," then followed with the admission that "I can't govern without you." In one short conciliatory meeting, Young had succeeded in cementing an alliance between city hall and business leaders that would remain strong throughout his terms in office.

At the same time that Young was solidifying his relationship with business leaders, he was working to diminish the influence of neighborhood groups by undermining the power of the NPU system. Under Young's administration, the NPU staff was reduced to one person, and in a series of stand-offs between business interests and neighborhood organizations, Young consistently weighed in on the side of business. In issues as diverse and as divisive as a proposal to create a "presidential parkway" in northeast Atlanta, a plan to establish an in-town "piggyback" facility to connect trucks (from I-20) with a CSX Transportation rail yard and line near the neighborhoods of Cabbagetown, Reynoldstown, and Grant Park, and the creation of a domed football stadium in the Vine City area, Mayor Young eventually supported the proposed projects despite the active and vocal opposition of neighborhood groups.

By the end of Young's first term of office, the relationship between business and city hall had been strengthened, and downtown business leaders once again had easy access to the mayor's office. But while this biracial coalition continued, the makeup of the local political power structure remained very different from that found in Atlanta during the early postwar decades. The office of the mayor, the presidency of the city council, and a large majority of Atlanta's elective and appointive offices were now held by African Americans, and the city that had been two-thirds white in 1950 was now two-thirds black. City hall remained pro-business and pro-development in its orientation, but the nature of those business connections was also changing. Andrew Young, for example, promoted Third World investment in the city and welcomed and encouraged an increasingly international business presence in Atlanta.

Young's mayoral administration was followed by the return of Maynard Jackson for a third term in office and, most recently, by Bill Campbell, a local black politician who had previously served the city for twelve years as a city council member. Despite these changes in administration, the basic outlines, priorities, and composition of the governing coalition has remained much the same over the past decade and a half.

A MODERN ECONOMY

TOURISM AND CONVENTIONS — The physical growth and expansion that the Atlanta metropolitan area experienced in the period from 1960 to 1990 was matched by an equally impressive expansion of the local economy. The second Forward Atlanta campaign of the early 1960s had succeeded in attracting new businesses to the city and had established Atlanta as the regional and national headquarters for a large number of Fortune 500 corporations. This influx of businesses and corporations, as noted earlier, augmented Atlanta's reputation as a commercial center and spurred construction and development in the downtown area.

In the 1970s, the growth industry for Atlanta and the surrounding region was the tourism and convention trade. In the downtown area alone, hotel room inventories increased from 4,000 in 1965 to 14,000 ten years later as more and more high-rise hotels were built to handle the rapidly increasing demand. By 1972, Atlanta already ranked third among cities in terms of its convention business, with only Chicago and New York handling more delegates per year.

"Spaghetti Junction," at the intersection of I-285 and I-85 in northeast Atlanta, where the city meets the suburbs. Everything on the left in the photo is "inside" the perimeter; everything on the right is "outside."

This dramatic growth in tourism was due to a number of factors. The Convention & Visitors Bureau's aggressive marketing of the city, for example, certainly helped, as did Atlanta's strategic transportation connections (including Hartsfield International Airport, links to three major interstate highways, and the city's long-established rail connections). But perhaps the biggest boost to the growth of the convention and tourist trade in the 1970s was the construction of hotels and support facilities to accommodate large conferences and trade shows. Chief among these new convention buildings were the Merchandise Mart (which opened in 1961 and was expanded in 1968); the Civic Auditorium (1965); the Apparel Mart (1979, expanded in 1989); the Omni International (an office-hotel megastructure that was completed in 1972); and the World Congress Center (which opened in 1976 and featured the nation's largest single-floor exhibition space and a large auditorium with built-in simultaneous interpretation facilities). These facilities (coupled with the presence of the city's various sports stadiums) not only enabled Atlanta to host innumerable conferences, conventions, concerts, and trade shows, but also brought high-profile events like the 1988 Democratic National Convention and the 1994 Super Bowl to the city.

THE GOVERNMENT PRESENCE — Also contributing significantly to the growth of the local economy since World War II have been a wide spectrum of governmental agencies and institutions based in the metropolitan area. Atlanta functions not only as the seat of municipal and county government, but also as the capital of the state. In addition, it is the locus of the largest concentration of federal governmental agencies (including the rapidly growing Centers for Disease Control and Prevention) outside Washington, D.C., and the site for a number of military bases and installations, including Dobbins Air Force Base, Fort McPherson, and the Atlanta Naval Air Station.

Taken as a whole, these governmental bodies constitute one of the metropolitan area's largest employers and a force that has exerted considerable influence in the last five decades on Atlanta's development and changing economy. In fact, with the increasing movement of jobs, retail industries, and office buildings to the urban perimeter, the government presence in downtown has proven to be one of the area's few stabilizing influences. And it is the federal government that is scheduled to take the place (both figuratively and literally) of one of downtown Atlanta's most important commercial institutions—Rich's department store.

THE INTERNATIONAL CITY — Throughout its history, Atlanta has invented slogans and visions to announce both its future aspirations and its heightened conceptions of its current importance. In the nineteenth century, the city advertised its role as "The Gateway to the South," and during the height of the Civil Rights Movement, Atlanta pronounced itself "The City Too Busy to Hate." In the early 1970s, the city elevated its status yet again to the level of "The World's Next Great City." And like the slogans of earlier eras, this latest proclamation was at first one part reality, two parts exaggeration.

In the years that followed, however, Atlanta gained additional support for its self-description as a city of international impor-

Atlanta's landmark department store, Rich's, shown in 1949 with the annual Christmas tree atop the bridge between the Store for Homes and the Store for Men. Downtown Rich's closed in 1991.

tance. The construction of the massive Hartsfield International Airport, for example, provided the city with international flight connections. And the opening of the World Congress Center and the construction of increasing numbers of high-rise hotels in downtown Atlanta and in the suburban periphery strengthened the city's hold on a rapidly increasing international convention business. International economic ties to Atlanta were also furthered through the arrival of foreign companies and investors in the metropolitan area. By 1995, there were more than 1,000 foreign companies from 35 foreign countries located in the Atlanta metropolitan statistical area, as well as 42 foreign consulates (career and honorary) and 27 trade and tourism offices.

The international presence in Atlanta has also increased through the arrival of new ethnic and immigrant groups. In March 1995, for example, there were an estimated 105,000 Hispanic residents in metropolitan Atlanta, some 25,000 Jamaicans, 13,000 Koreans, and almost 20,000 immigrants and refugees from southeast Asia. (Despite this influx, Atlanta's dominant population groups continue to be African Americans and whites.)

At the same time that international groups and businesses were establishing a presence in Atlanta, Atlanta-based businesses, organizations, and even sports teams were increasing their visibility abroad. Coca-Cola, for example, built upon its World War II overseas expansion to become perhaps the most recognized commercial product in the world, and Cable News Network (CNN), a locally based creation of Turner Broadcasting, emerged as the world's most-watched news network. Former president Jimmy Carter has expanded Atlanta's international visibility through the efforts of the Carter Center to negotiate for peace and to eradicate the crippling effects of poverty and disease in countries all over the globe. And Atlanta's first major league professional sports team—the Atlanta Braves—became the National League Champions in 1991 and 1992 and the World Baseball Champions in 1995 (forever erasing the sports image of Atlanta as "Loserville").

Of course, the event that may have the greatest impact on Atlanta, to cement its status as a truly international city, is the

1996 Centennial Olympic Games. The Olympics promise to draw millions of new visitors to the city and to establish international connections that will survive long after the games. The impact of the Olympics on the landscape and structure of Atlanta may be equally dramatic. A new Olympic stadium, for example, has been built in the community of Summerhill (in the same area where residents were displaced some thirty years earlier during construction of the Atlanta–Fulton County Stadium); the Olympic Village, which will house the athletes, has been constructed in the midst of the Georgia Tech campus and Techwood Homes (the nation's first public housing project); and a Centennial Olympic Park in downtown Atlanta is being established to provide a gathering place for Olympic visitors and to spark change, growth, and development in the city's center. Whether this Olympics-related growth and expansion merely accelerates metropolitan trends already in progress in Atlanta or alters them in new and dramatic ways remains to be seen.

CONCLUSION

During the last half of the twentieth century, the Atlanta metropolitan region has undergone revolutionary changes in its boundaries, its economic and political structure, and its racial composition. The expansion of the region's highways and the relocation of industries and businesses to outlying areas have drawn the metropolitan population with it, and, lacking topographical barriers, Atlanta has grown far beyond its original borders, bumping up against its rural neighbors and creating "edge cities" where employment, shopping malls, and residences are clustered. (Indeed, portions of the Atlanta countryside have gone from rural to suburban without ever passing through an urban phase.) These suburban communities are now not only the centers of growth in the metropolitan region but the residential locus of the majority of Atlanta's white citizens.

Within the city limits, on the other hand, Atlanta's central business district has been reshaped through urban renewal and highway construction, and the city's population has been transformed from majority white to majority black. Accompanying this change in the racial composition of the city has been an equally dramatic alteration in the makeup of the political power structure. The postwar governing coalition in which the dominant partners were white mayors and the white business elite has given way to a new power structure in which white business leaders still retain influence but African Americans hold the majority of the city's elective and appointive offices.

While these changes were taking place in metropolitan Atlanta, the region accumulated the accoutrements of a modern metropolis. Its population grew to several million. Professional sports teams were brought to the city. Atlanta's cultural organizations matured and became nationally recognized. A rapid transit system was built. The city skyline was expanded through the construction of high-rise buildings and skyscrapers. And a thriving tourism and convention industry transformed the downtown economy.

Despite these celebrated developments, the future progress of the region may depend on Atlanta's ability to bridge the racial and economic divide that separates city from suburb and to establish intraregional processes and agencies to plan and develop future metropolitan growth. The city of Atlanta's residents (totaling about 394,000 in 1990) are but a small component of the larger metropolitan area's population of more than 2.8 million. Similarly, the city itself is rather small in area (131.6 square miles), while the Atlanta metropolitan region is one of the largest in the Southeast. (The Atlanta Regional Commission defines the Atlanta "region" as a 10-county area encompassing 2,989 square miles and 64 cities. The "Atlanta Metropolitan Statistical Area," as defined by the U.S. Census Bureau, is even larger and includes 20 counties and a 6,126-square-mile area.)

Nonetheless, decisions made in the city of Atlanta continue to have a major impact on the larger metropolitan area; indeed, issues such as water treatment and conservation, the expansion of MARTA rail lines, road and highway construction, zoning regulations, and the building of new sports and entertainment facilities transcend municipal boundaries. Similarly, decisions made in Atlanta's growing suburban metropolis have the potential of dramatically affecting the city and its urban infrastructure.

If the suburban metropolis of Atlanta is to continue its impressive rate of growth in the future while the city maintains its status as a vital and successful conference, government, business, and entertainment center, some new means and agencies of intraregional cooperation and planning must clearly be established. How well Atlanta accomplishes these tasks may, in the final analysis, be determined by the region's success in overcoming the racial divisions, both social and geographical, that have historically segregated the city. If it is able to accomplish this goal, "The World's Next Great City" may well become "The Metropolis of Tomorrow."

Resources and Suggested Readings

GENERAL READINGS ON ATLANTA

Garrett, Franklin M. *Atlanta and Environs: A Chronicle of Its People and Events.* 2 vols. Athens: University of Georgia Press, 1954.

Kuhn, Clifford M., Harlon E. Joye, and E. Bernard West. *Living Atlanta: An Oral History of the City, 1914–1948.* Athens: University of Georgia Press, 1990.

Metropolitan Frontiers: Atlanta, 1835–2000. Permanent exhibition. Atlanta History Center. Opened 1993.

Russell, James Michael. *Atlanta, 1847–1890: City Building in the Old South and the New.* Baton Rouge: Louisiana State University Press, 1988.

Shavin, Norman, and Bruce Galphin. *Atlanta: Triumph of a People.* Atlanta: Capricorn Corp., 1982.

White, Dana F., and Timothy J. Crimmins, eds. *Atlanta Historical Journal* (Summer/Fall 1982). Special issue on the physical development of the city and surrounding areas.

ATLANTA: THE HEART OF A RURAL REGION, C. 1800–1865

"Atlanta's First Historical Society: 'The Atlanta Pioneer and Historic Society.'" Reprint from C. R. *Hanleiter's Directory of Atlanta*, 1871. Atlanta Historical Bulletin 1, no. 1 (Sept. 1927): 14–27.

Barker, Meta, comp. "Some Proceedings of the Atlanta City Council, 1848–1861." *Atlanta Historical Bulletin* 2 (July 1937): 27–35.

Ehle, John. *The Trail of Tears: The Rise and Fall of the Cherokee Nation.* New York: Anchor Books/Doubleday, 1988.

Francis, Hubert C. "The Origin of Fulton County." *Atlanta Historical Bulletin* 13 (September 1968): 72–80.

Garrow, Patrick H. *The Archaeology of DeKalb County: A Summary.* Garrow & Associates, Inc., 1989.

Goff, John. *Placenames in Georgia: Essays of John Goff.* Edited by Francis Lee Utley and Marion Hemperley. Athens: University of Georgia Press, 1975.

Harrison, John M. "The Irish Influence in Early Atlanta."
Paper presented at a meeting of the Atlanta Historical
Society, September 30, 1944.

Hudson, Charles. *The Southeastern Indians.* Knoxville:
University of Tennessee Press, 1976.

Humphries, John D. "The Organization of DeKalb County."
Atlanta Historical Bulletin 8 (December 1947): 17–30.

Kurtz, Wilbur. "Standing Peachtree." *Early Georgia* 1
(1950): 31–42.

———. "The Story of Land Lot 77—Atlanta." *Atlanta
Historical Bulletin* 8, no. 32 (December 1947): 42–67.

"Metropolitan Frontiers: Atlanta, 1835–2000." Exhibition
research files. Atlanta History Center.

Mitchell, Eugene M. "Atlanta's First Real-Estate Subdivision
and Other Curious Facts About the Early History of
Atlanta. *Atlanta Historical Bulletin* 1, no. 3 (May 1930):
7–14.

Newman, Harvey. "Some Reflections on Religion in
Nineteenth-Century Atlanta: A Research Note." *Atlanta
Historical Journal* 27 (Fall 1983): 47–56.

Pioneer Citizens History of Atlanta, 1833–1902. Atlanta:
Byrd Printing Co., 1902.

Sherwood, Rev. Adiel A. M. *A Gazetteer of the State of
Georgia.* 1827. Reprint, Athens: University of Georgia
Press, 1939.

Shingleton, Royce. *Richard Peters: Champion of the New
South.* Macon, Georgia: Mercer University Press, 1985.

"Snake Nation." Subject files. Library/Archives. Atlanta
History Center, Library/Archives.

White, Dana F., and Timothy J. Crimmins, "Atlanta at 150."
Atlanta Journal-Constitution, October 4, 1987.

Atlanta: An Emerging Transportation Center, 1865–1900

Atlanta Exposition and South Illustrated. Chicago: Adler Art
Publishing Co., 1895.

Ayers, Edward L. *The Promise of the New South: Life After Reconstruction*. New York and Oxford: Oxford University Press, 1992.

Beard, Rick E. "From Suburb to Defended Neighborhood: Change in Atlanta's Inman Park and Ansley Park, 1890–1980." *Atlanta Historical Journal* 26 (Summer-Fall 1982): 113–40.

Carson, O. E. *The Trolley Titans*. Glendale, California: Interurban Press, 1981.

Carter, Rev. E. R. *The Black Side: A Partial History of the Business, Religious and Educational Side of the Negro in Atlanta*. Atlanta: n. p., 1894.

Castel, Albert. *Decision in the West: The Atlanta Campaign of 1864*. Lawrence: University Press of Kansas, 1992.

Coca-Cola Company. *The Coca-Cola Company: A Chronological History, 1886–1971*. Atlanta: The Coca-Cola Company, 1971.

Cooper, Walter G. *The Cotton States and International Exposition and South, Illustrated*. Atlanta: The Illustrator Co., 1896.

Garrett, Franklin. *Yesterday's Atlanta*. Miami: E. A. Seemann Publishing, Inc., 1977.

Grady, Henry. *The New South*. Biographical sketch by Oliver Dyer. New York: Robert Bonner's Sons, 1890.

Hertzberg, Steven. "The Jewish Community of Atlanta from the End of the Civil War Until the Eve of the Frank Case." *American Jewish Historical Quarterly* 62 (March 1973): 250–85.

———. *Strangers Within the Gate City: The Jews of Atlanta, 1845–1915*. Philadelphia: Jewish Publication Society of America, 1978.

Hitt, Michael D. *After the Left Flank: Military Operations in the Roswell Area after July 16, 1864, and the Journey of the Roswell Mill Employees*. Privately printed, 1985.

Hodler, Thomas W., and Howard A. Schretter. *The Atlas of Georgia*. Athens: University of Georgia, Institute of Community and Area Development, 1986.

King, Augusta Wylie. "Atlanta's First Ball Park and Baseball Team, 1866." *Atlanta Historical Bulletin* 8 (December 1947): 12–17.

Sheehan, C. J. "Atlanta's Public Schools, 1873–1883." *Atlanta Historical Bulletin* 2 (November 1936): 5–12.

Shingleton, Royce. *Richard Peters*. Macon, Georgia: Mercer University Press, 1985.

Sparks, Andrew. "The College That Began in a Boxcar and a Basement." *Atlanta Journal-Constitution Magazine*, August 15, 1965.

Stanley, Raymond Wallace. "The Railroad Pattern of Atlanta." Master's thesis. University of Chicago, 1947.

"The State Capitol of Georgia." Pamphlet. Subject files. Atlanta History Center, Library/Archives.

Thornberry, Jerry John. "The Development of Black Atlanta, 1865—1885." Ph.D. diss. University of Maryland, 1977.

Watts, Eugene J. "Black Political Progress in Atlanta: 1868–1895." *Journal of Negro History* 59 (July 1974): 268–86.

White, Dana F., and Timothy J. Crimmins. "Atlanta at 150." *Atlanta Journal-Constitution*, October 4, 1987.

———. "How Atlanta Grew: Cool Heads, Hot Air, and Hard Work." *Atlanta Economic Review* 28, no. 1 (January-February 1978): 7–15.

ATLANTA: THE COMMERCIAL CITY, 1900–1940

Brownell, Blaine A. "The Commercial-Civic Elite and City Planning in Atlanta, Memphis and New Orleans in the 1920s." *Journal of Southern History* 41 (August 1975): 339–68.

Bryant, James C. "Yaarab Temple and the Fox Theatre: The Survival of a Dream." *Atlanta History: A Journal of Georgia and the South* 39 (Summer 1995): 5–22.

Burrison, John A. "Fiddlers in the Alley: Atlanta as an Early Country Music Center." *Atlanta Historical Bulletin* 21 (Summer 1977): 59–87.

Crimmins, Timothy J. "Bungalow Suburbs: East and West."

Atlanta Historical Journal 26 (Summer-Fall 1982): 83–94.

Dinnerstein, Leonard. *The Leo Frank Case.* New York: Columbia University Press, 1968.

Dittmer, John. *Black Georgia in the Progressive Era.* Urbana: University of Illinois Press, 1977.

Fleming, Douglas L. "The New Deal in Atlanta: A Review of the Major Programs." *Atlanta Historical Journal* 30 (Spring 1986): 23–45.

Goodson, Steve. "This Mighty Influence for Good and Evil: The Movies in Atlanta, 1895–1920." *Atlanta History: A Journal of Georgia and the South* 39 (Fall-Winter 1995): 28–47.

Grantham, Dewey W. "Regional Claims and National Purposes: The South and the New Deal." *Atlanta History: A Journal of Georgia and the South* 38 (Fall 1994): 5–17.

Hall, Jacquelyn Dowd. "Private Eyes, Public Women: Images of Class and Sex in the Urban South, Atlanta, Georgia, 1913–1915." *Atlanta History: A Journal of Georgia and the South* 36 (Winter 1993): 24–39.

———. *Revolt Against Chivalry: Jessie Daniel Ames and the Women's Campaign Against Lynching.* New York: Columbia University Press, 1979.

Herring, Neill, and Sue Thrasher. "UAW Sit-down Strike, Atlanta, 1936." *Southern Exposure* 1 (Winter 1974): 63–83.

Hertzberg, Steven. *Strangers Within the Gate City: The Jews of Atlanta, 1845–1915.* Philadelphia: Jewish Publishing Society of America, 1978.

Jackson, Kenneth T. *The Ku Klux Klan in the City.* New York: Oxford University Press, 1967.

Maclachlan, Gretchen E. "Atlanta's Industrial Women, 1879–1920." *Atlanta History: A Journal of Georgia and the South* 36 (Winter 1993): 16–23.

Martin, Charles H. *The Angelo Herndon Case and Southern Justice.* Baton Rouge: Louisiana State University Press, 1978.

Matthews, John Michael. "The Georgia 'Race Strike' of 1909." *Journal of Southern History* 40 (November 1974): 613–30.

Moseley, Charlton. "William Joseph Simmons: The Unknown Wizard." *Atlanta History: A Journal of Georgia and the South* 37 (Spring 1993): 17–32.

Preston, Howard L. *Automobile Age Atlanta: The Making of a Southern Metropolis*. Athens: University of Georgia Press, 1979.

Pomerantz, Gary. *Where Peachtree Meets Sweet Auburn*. New York: Scribner, 1996.

Roth, Darlene Rebecca. *Matronage: Patterns in Women's Organizations, Atlanta, Georgia, 1890–1940*. New York: Carlson Publishing Inc., 1994.

Rouse, Jacqueline Anne. *Lugenia Burns Hope: Black Southern Reformer*. Athens: University of Georgia Press, 1989.

Watson-Powers, Lynn. "Southern Bases: Baseball Before the Braves." *Atlanta History: A Journal of Georgia and the South* 37 (Summer 1993): 25–40.

White, Dana F. "The Black Sides of Atlanta: A Geography of Expansion and Containment, 1970–1870." *Atlanta Historical Journal* 26 (Summer-Fall 1982): 199–225.

Wiggins, Gene. *Fiddlin' Georgia Crazy: Fiddlin' John Carson, His Real World and the World of His Songs*. Urbana: University of Illinois Press, 1987.

Atlanta: A Suburban Metropolis, 1940–1996

Allen, Frederick. *Atlanta Rising: The Invention of an International City, 1946–1996*. Atlanta: Longstreet Press, 1996.

Allen, Ivan, Jr., and Paul Hemphill. *Mayor: Notes on the Sixties*. Athens: University of Georgia Press, 1978.

Ambrose, Andy. "Redrawing the Color Line: The History and Patterns of Black Housing in Atlanta, 1940–1973." Ph.D. diss. Emory University, 1992.

Bayor, Ronald H. *Race and the Shaping of Twentieth-Century Atlanta*. Athens: University of Georgia Press, 1996.

———. "Roads to Racial Segregation: Atlanta in the

Twentieth Century." *Journal of Urban History* 15:1 (November 1988): 3–21.

Bullard, Robert D., and E. Kiki Thomas. "Atlanta: Mecca of the Southeast." In *In Search of the New South: Black Urban Experiences in the 1970s and 1980s*, edited by Robert D. Bullard, 75–97. Tuscaloosa: University of Alabama Press, 1989.

Crowe, Charles. "Racial Massacre in Atlanta, September 22, 1906." *Journal of Negro History* 54 (April 1969): 150–73.

Egerton, John. *Speak Now Against the Day: The Generation Before the Civil Rights Movement in the South*. New York: Knopf, 1994.

Fairclough, Adam. *To Redeem the Soul of America: The Southern Christian Leadership Conference and Martin Luther King, Jr.* Athens: University of Georgia Press, 1987.

Garreau, Joel. "Atlanta: The Color of Money." In *Edge City: Life on the New Frontier*, 139–78. New York: Doubleday, 1991.

Goldfield, David R. *Black, White, and Southern: Race Relations and Southern Culture, 1940 to the Present*. Baton Rouge: Louisiana State University Press, 1990.

Hampton, Henry, and Steve Fayer. *Voices of Freedom: An Oral History of the Civil Rights Movements from the 1950s through the 1980s*. New York: Bantam Books, 1990.

Hein, Virginia H. "The Image of a City Too Busy to Hate: Atlanta in the 1960s." *Phylon* 33 (Fall 1972): 205–21.

Hornsby, Alton, Jr. "The Negro in Atlanta Politics, 1961–1973." *Atlanta Historical Bulletin* 21 (Spring 1977): 9–11.

King, Coretta Scott. *My Life with Martin Luther King, Jr.* New York: Holt, Rineholt, and Winston, 1969.

Rice, Bradley R. "If Atlanta Were Dixie." In *Sunbelt Cities: Politics and Growth Since World War II*, edited by Richard R. Bernedad and Bradley R. Rice, 31–57. Austin: University of Texas Press, 1983.

Schwartz, Janet, and Denise Black. *Ethnic Atlanta*. Atlanta: Longstreet Press, 1993.

Silver, Christopher, and John V. Moeser. *The Separate City: Black Communities in the Urban South, 1940–1968.* Lexington: University Press of Kentucky, 1995.

Stone, Clarence N. *Regime Politics: Governing Atlanta, 1946–1988.* Lawrence: University Press of Kansas, 1989.

Thompson, Robert A., Hylan Lewis, and Davis McEntire. "Atlanta and Birmingham: A Comparative Study in Negro Housing." In *Housing and Minority Groups*, edited by Nathan Glazer and Davis McEntire, 13–83. Berkeley: University of California Press, 1960.